REACHING AND TEACHING THROUGH EDUCATIONAL PSYCHOTHERAPY

D1477857

REACHING AND TEACHING THROUGH EDUCATIONAL PSYCHOTHERAPY

A Case Study Approach

By

GILLIAN SALMON & JENNY DOVER

LEARNING RESOURCES CENTRE
Havering College
of Further and Higher education

John Wiley & Sons, Ltd

Other Wiley Editorial Offices

John Wiley & Sons Inc., 111 River Street, Hoboken, NJ 07030, USA

Jossey-Bass, 989 Market Street, San Francisco, CA 94103-1741, USA

Wiley-VCH Verlag GmbH, Boschstr. 12, D-69469 Weinheim, Germany

John Wiley & Sons Australia Ltd, 42 McDougall Street, Milton, Queensland 4064, Australia

John Wiley & Sons (Asia) Pte Ltd, 2 Clementi Loop #02-01, Jin Xing Distripark, Singapore 129809

John Wiley & Sons Canada Ltd, 6045 Freemont Blvd, Mississauga, ONT, L5R 4J3, Canada

Wiley also publishes its books in a variety of electronic formats. Some content that appears in print may not be
available in electronic books.

Anniversary Logo Design: Richard J. Pacifico

Library of Congress Cataloging-in-Publication Data

Salmon, Gillian.
  Reaching and teaching through educational therapy : a case study approach / by Gillian Salmon & Jenny Dover.
    p. cm.
  Includes bibliographical references and index.
  ISBN 978-0-470-51299-9 (pbk.)
  1. Remedial teaching. 2. Learning disabled children–Education. 3. Learning disabled children–
Education–Great Britain–Case studies. 4. School psychology. I. Dover, Jenny. II. Title.
  LB1029.R4S24 2007
  371.9–dc22

                                                   2007014667

A catalogue record for this book is available from the British Library

ISBN: 978-0-470-51299-9

Typeset by Thomson Press (India) Limted
Printed and bound in Great Britain by TJ International, Padstow.
This book is printed on acid-free paper responsibly manufactured from sustainable forestry in which at least two
trees are planted for each one used for paper production.

Contents

Acknowledgements

This book is constructed around the four case studies written by teachers who were training in educational psychotherapy. We are very grateful to the following:

- Patricia Reid – Educational Psychotherapist working in a mainstream school
- Merkel Sender – Senior Educational Psychologist in Waltham Forest
- Claire Warner – Head of Social, Emotional and Behavioural Support Service
- Dorothy Wickson – Educational Psychotherapist.

for their permission to use accounts of the clinical work they undertook while in training. We would also like to acknowledge the important contribution to educational psychotherapy made by those organizing and teaching on the training courses, the students who have taken part in the training and the many other people who have supported the work of the Caspari Foundation.

1 Introduction

Inclusion has become an educational term. It implies that all children benefit from the opportunity to engage, with a wide range of their peers, in the learning situation, but also that some of them have greater difficulty than others in doing so. For a teacher, this can present an enormous challenge if she is confronted with a child who neither responds to the teaching approaches used in the classroom, nor to the support available from the special needs staff. The teacher is often left with a bewildering sense that there is something underlying the child's difficulty that has not been identified and that, if only it were, she would be able to work more successfully with the child.

A five-year old boy was becoming more and more difficult to handle in school, was refusing to learn and was extremely difficult to engage in any tasks. He roamed the classroom projecting angry and aggressive feelings towards other children (pushing, swearing, spitting, hitting, kicking and punching) and subsequently hitting out at the adults working with him. Both at school and at home he was described as aggressive, wilful and impervious to boundary setting. His teacher was able to recognize his insecurity and anxiety and she described him as an 'emotional child needing constant affirmation of his mum's love' as having 'a lot of things on his mind' and being 'often distracted'. Recognition of the link between emotional problems and difficulties with learning often gives teachers the feeling that the two could be addressed simultaneously, but does not necessarily give teachers a clear insight into how this might be done.

Educational psychotherapy, as its name implies, is a fusion of educational and therapeutic techniques and insights. This approach was developed by the late Irene Caspari, who was Principal Psychologist at the Tavistock Clinic between the 1950s and 1970s. The training that has evolved from this work is mentioned in the conclusion. In 2007, a decision was made to change the term 'educational therapy' as used since the time of Irene Caspari, to 'educational psychotherapy'. It was considered by members of the Caspari Foundation that this was a more accurate term for the way of working and this is therefore the term used throughout this book. In this book we introduce the reader to ways in which an educational psychotherapist can work to address educational difficulties alongside the emotional problems that underlie the learning problems. By quoting detailed examples of intensive work with children in either school or clinic, we hope to give a vivid impression of what it is like to be with a child in educational psychotherapy. Of course, teachers will be aware of other approaches to understanding children's learning difficulties. The case studies show this particular approach in action. Alongside the case studies we give accounts of some practical aspects of the work and some of the theoretical ideas that support it. We should make clear that, except when we are referring to specific instances in the work with Maria, the only girl described, we use the pronouns 'she' for the teacher and 'he' for the child, in an effort at greater clarity.

Most teachers, while recognizing the gains that a child may make from such an intervention as educational psychotherapy, also realize that, as described in these case studies, this is a clinical approach that is not always available to the child who needs it. Neither is it appropriate for a teacher who has a particular role in the school to carry out therapeutic work of such intensity. There are, however, many ways in which teaching, either individually, small group or classroom teaching can use the insights and some of the techniques that make teaching therapeutic. We hope to draw out of some of the examples described, an understanding of the processes involved and the ways in which these can be applied to working with children in the classroom.

Teachers who are interested in this way of working will find that it is relevant to all phases of education and any type of school or unit and that the insights gained from studying the educational psychotherapy approach can be applied to children of any age or ability.

The case studies quoted in this book have been written by experienced teachers who were educational psychotherapists in training and are summaries of the background to the work, the way in which the therapy developed and the child's response to it. The reader may not be surprised to find that, of the four case studies, three describe work with boys and only one of them is an account of work with a girl. It has long been a concern that more boys than girls tend to be identified as having special educational needs and these cases reflect the proportions in which this often happens. The reader will also note that the children are drawn from diverse cultural backgrounds and that an important part of the work has been to try to engage their parents in supporting the work with their child. The majority of cases quoted also tend to be of work with primary age children. Although older children are often referred for educational psychotherapy, and can be appropriately worked with, there is often a perception that the younger child may be able to make better use of such an intervention and that there is more time available for intensive work. It is also the case that many of the insights gained from work with younger children can be applied to teenagers and we hope to indicate a number of these.

The case studies were chosen to illustrate a range of emotional problems within the families and the ways in which the children's past experience impacted upon their capacity to learn. Each child is stuck in a particular response to a learning opportunity and so the capacity of each child to make use of the opportunity is compromised. The case studies also explore what it is like to be an adult engaged with a child who is having difficulty in learning and how this can be reflected in the difficulty the therapist has in learning how to be therapeutic. It is often the case that, when reading accounts of therapeutic work, the therapist seems to know what to do as if by 'magic'. We hope that, by using accounts of work done while the therapists were in the early stages of developing their skills, the reader will understand something of that learning process and feel able to share the feeling of 'not knowing' but being able to 'think about' the child.

Among the important insights used in this work are an understanding of the way in which a child may transfer feelings from early relationships with carers to the adult teaching him. The teacher also brings feelings to the work with the child. These derive from her own early experience as well as from her unconscious response to what the child brings. These theoretical concepts, and others which derive from psychoanalytic and attachment theory and are particularly useful in understanding a child's response to the teaching and learning situation, are explained in Chapter 7. The use of the metaphor in exploring the feelings revealed in the work is described together with other techniques and materials that are found to be effective in working with children in educational psychotherapy. Chapter 3 details the process of assessment and considers ways in which the child's approach to the task and response to creative activities can inform the teacher about the nature of the difficulties.

Each child has also attracted the concern of teachers and other professionals and we attempt to put into perspective, in Chapter 10, some of the issues that arise when adults work together in the interests of the child. The importance to the work of the way in which it is set up and the structures and boundaries that support it are considered in Chapters 5 and 9. We hope that, by the end of the book, the reader will be familiar with some of the ways in which a therapeutic approach can be taken to addressing the emotional problems that often impede a child's learning.

2 Case Study of Osman, A Withdrawn Child Who Cannot Make Connections

This first case study is written by Merkel Sender and describes the work with Osman who was referred for educational psychotherapy when he was eight years old. Of all the children discussed in the studies Osman is the least emotionally and cognitively mature and has little sense of himself as a separate individual with his own valid thoughts and feelings. His psychotherapist notes his fear of 'both people and things', his incapacity to engage in imaginary play and his difficulty in emotionally connecting with her. The account of the work illustrates the way in which missing out on positive attachment experiences as an infant affects a child's later learning. With this in mind the psychotherapist attempts to offer Osman a second opportunity for learning. Over time, she is able to give him an experience of someone who can understand and bear his powerful feelings, strengthen his self-awareness and create a safe enough environment for being curious and thinking. The study also illustrates how the educational and play activities themselves provide an opportunity for a child to express and explore experiences as well as offering an indirect means of engaging with the therapist.

INTRODUCTION

This is an account of the work with a boy who was seen for educational psychotherapy, with supervision, for two school years between the ages of 8 years 1 month and 9 years 10 months. The work took place in a Child and Adolescent Mental Health Service (CAMHS) clinic. We worked in a large room furnished with a carpet, a desk, some chairs and a small table and chair. Other than a doll's house, which was placed out of reach on top of a built-in cupboard, there was nothing else in the room. During the second year we worked in a smaller room that had a carpet, a small table, some chairs, a bed and an empty sand tray. Most of the materials used were kept in a box, which I took into each session. A variety of other materials such as number games, painting materials, reading books, word games, were brought to the sessions when it was considered appropriate to do so.

FAMILY BACKGROUND

Osman is an only child who lives at home with his parents, in a self-contained flat, in a house that is shared with some members of the extended family. The family is of

Turkish origin and both Turkish and English are spoken at home. Father came to this country as a young child and speaks English more fluently than mother, who arrived here in her teens. Father at present works as a mini-cab driver and mother works part-time from home as a dressmaker. When I started working with Osman, his father was in his late thirties and mother was eight years younger. The family's main social context is their own extended family. Osman does not have any friends outside the family; all the while I worked with him no one was invited to tea, and Osman himself was only invited out once, to the birthday party of a child in his class.

OSMAN'S EARLY HISTORY

According to the clinic notes, which do not provide a great deal of information, Osman's parents considered him to be 'a good baby'. They reported that he would not breast feed and refused solids when they were first offered at two to three months. He walked at about 13 months and there were no problems with toilet training. No reference is made to early language development.

Osman's general health was good, although from the age of two-and-a-half years he appears to have had recurrent middle-ear infections, which resulted in his having an operation at about four years old to have grommets inserted. There have been no problems since then and his hearing is normal.

When Osman was born, his parents were living in a flat above a restaurant, which they managed. Financial considerations made it necessary for mother to return to work when Osman was about a year old. She worked extremely long hours and he was looked after by a succession of young girls, most of whom, according to the parents, were 'quite hopeless'. In an interview with the child psychiatrist, his mother remarked that this experience had had an effect on Osman and that when she was able to be with him he showed no interest in her, nor did he play with toys.

REFERRAL PROCESS

Osman's behaviour caused concern when he began attending the nursery department in an infant school. The nursery staff described him as a child who was unwilling to communicate verbally, who did not make eye contact and who rarely interacted with other children or adults. According to the nursery staff his mother rarely visited and, when she did, she gave them the impression of being depressed.

There was no noticeable improvement in his behaviour when he transferred to the reception class. His teacher described him as reticent, particularly with adults, and considered that some of his abilities were delayed although the notes do not go into any detail about this. His difficulties were discussed with the educational psychologist during Osman's first term in the reception class. He undertook to monitor Osman's progress. At about the same time the hospital teacher of the deaf who was assessing Osman's hearing in relation to his early ear infections and subsequent hospital admission, referred him for a speech therapy assessment. His hearing was normal, but he was not talking.

The speech therapy assessment revealed that his language skills were probably average but that he was withholding speech in situations other than at home. His problem was diagnosed as a difficulty in relating to other people. Following the assessment, Osman received speech therapy from the hospital for a year, between the ages of five-and-a-half and six-and-a-half years. During this time a clinical psychologist also saw the family following a referral, presumably by the speech therapist, to the hospital's child psychiatric department. Osman responded well to speech therapy on an individual basis but this progress was not reflected at school where he reverted to noncommunicative behaviour when he moved into the middle infants at six years of age. Both the speech therapist and the educational psychologist considered it unlikely that Osman had genuine language problems or low overall ability and felt it was more likely that his psychological problems were preventing him from cooperating in situations where demands were placed on him.

Speech therapy was resumed at a local clinic after a six-month delay. At this stage Osman was just seven years old and he was seen by the local speech therapist for 10 months. She, too, felt that his problems were primarily of a psychological nature. She was particularly concerned about his difficulty in separating from his father during speech therapy sessions. She obtained parental consent, while she was still working with Osman, to refer the family to the CAMHS clinic. They were seen by a social worker and offered family therapy, which they declined.

In view of Osman's lack of progress in basic skills at school, other than mechanical reading, and his difficulty in working or socializing with other children, a decision was made during the summer term to transfer him to an opportunity class rather than the junior school, at the beginning of the next school year. Opportunity classes, which cater for a maximum of 10 children, are situated in mainstream schools. Each class has a teacher and a full-time welfare assistant. These classes aim to provide more specialized individual teaching for children with learning difficulties and also concentrate on developing social skills in order to enable the children to return to mainstream education after one or two years.

During the summer term the educational psychologist again referred the family to CAMHS. Osman's parents were seen by the consultant child psychiatrist and Osman was seen individually by her as well. In view of his extreme distress in separating from his father during the interview, the child psychiatrist did not feel that it would be appropriate to offer him individual psychotherapy. Following a discussion between the parents and the child psychiatrist, Osman was referred to me for educational psychotherapy a few weeks after he began attending the opportunity class.

I was introduced to the parents by the child psychiatrist at a meeting held a few days before I was due to meet Osman. At this meeting, I was able to explain what educational psychotherapy might be able to offer Osman and to obtain some idea of the parents' views of his needs. His mother appeared shy and less communicative than his father, who did most of the talking. He expressed considerable concern about Osman's lack of progress at school. 'He's a clever boy. I don't know what's holding him back.' Father admitted to other anxieties. He felt that Osman had 'no personality of his own', that instead of developing his own personality he mimicked his father. Both parents expressed considerable anxiety about whether or not Osman would be able to separate from his father, who would be bringing him to his sessions as mother did not drive.

FIRST SESSION

I first met Osman in the clinic waiting room when he came for his first session accompanied by his father. My initial impression was of a chubby, listless, lumpish child with a sallow complexion, large brown eyes and longish black hair. In view of his anticipated difficulty in separating from father I invited them both to come upstairs with me to the room where Osman and I would be working. With encouragement from his father and me, Osman sat down on a chair next to a small table, on which I had placed a box containing a variety of materials for his use. I sat beside him and at my suggestion father sat on the other side of the room. Osman perched on the edge of the chair, ill at ease, with an anxious expression on his face. He didn't look at me at all throughout the session. He ignored my suggestion that he might like to take off his anorak and did not respond to any of the neutral questions that I asked about school, except to whisper his teacher's name. Father, who, perhaps like me, was finding this withdrawn behaviour discomfiting, often answered for him.

When I drew Osman's attention to what I called his 'special box' and wondered whether he might like to find out what was inside it, he nodded, almost imperceptibly. This glimmer of interest made me feel that this was an opportune moment to ask father to wait downstairs. As father left the room Osman's facial expression became even more dejected. He uttered an almost inaudible 'no' and his eyes filled with tears. However he did not cry and was able to remain in the room with me for about 35 minutes. While looking at the contents of his box he made no attempt to get anything out himself but did appear interested in some of the things for example stapler, paper punch. He used gestures rather than words to express his interest. Although he didn't initiate any conversation he answered in whispered monosyllables some of the questions I asked. I found his behaviour made me feel anxious and inadequate.

What came across so powerfully in this first session was Osman's lack of spontaneity and the feeling I had that for him both things and people were frightening. To give one example: 'I can't do it' he whispered, as he attempted to cut around a simple pattern we had made using the paper punch. He was in fact able to cut well – when gently encouraged. I was aware, too, of the effect of his anxiety on his thought and language processes. He was unable to count out four objects correctly and, when I showed him some animals in his box, he seemed unable to name them, but said repeatedly 'I know . . . I know.'

I had anticipated separation difficulties at the second session, especially as this took place after the half-term holiday, but Osman evidently did not find me threatening and came upstairs with me while his father remained in the waiting room. Separating from father did not subsequently cause him any anxiety and as the sessions continued there were no problems when father made it obvious that he would be leaving the premises while Osman was with me. The fact that he had been able to stay with me during the initial session was important not only for Osman but for his parents as well as it gave them some confidence in my ability to work with him. Father, at later meetings, referred to the initial session as a 'major breakthrough'.

Expression work and play: omnipotence, lack of initiative, unrelatedness

Osman communicated very little verbally during the first term, and for the first five weeks relied almost exclusively on nonverbal gestures to make his needs known. However, his behaviour made me aware of his need to be in control, his 'omnipotent' phantasy that he did not need to be dependent.

I brought the game of Connect to the second session and, as Osman seemed interested, I helped him assemble the frame. He then proceeded, slowly and carefully to drop the counters into the frame, one yellow counter followed by a red one, until the supply was exhausted. He misplaced one of the counters but ignored me when I suggested that he look at his pattern once it was completed. He then tipped all the counters out of the frame and repeated the activity. When he began to repeat the activity a third time I joined in and altered the pattern slightly, but he ignored this and continued with his pattern when it was his turn. Although he concentrated hard and was absorbed in what he was doing, the repetitive, almost obsessional way in which he emptied and filled the frame had a mindless quality about it. I felt shut out – where there should have been a feeling of shared space there was nothing. There were no connections. Osman was filling up the space himself.

Throughout the term there were numerous examples of Osman's need to be in control. At one session I introduced a simple number activity, which involved matching numbers to counters. Osman enjoyed this until I pointed out a mistake. He immediately said that he didn't want to do it anymore; he would 'leave it for next week'. This did not suggest to me any sense of continuity about the sessions but rather his need to be omnipotent. It was unbearable for him to be helped because that implied not knowing and it seemed that, for Osman, not knowing aroused feelings of helplessness.

In many ways Osman's play with the animals during the first term displayed the same qualities of omnipotence and also his reluctance to take the initiative. During the third session he intimated that he would like to play with the animals and I suggested that he might like to join the plastic fences. He made a half-hearted attempt to do so but gave up very quickly. The fences connected in a similar way to the parts of the Connect frame and his inability to join them suggested to me that he had difficulty in making use of his experience and needed to go back to the beginning each time. Perhaps, too, his inability to join things reflected his fragile ego relatedness. He was, however, able to join the fences once I showed him what to do and he made a square, which he then filled with as many animals as possible. Having done this, he removed the animals and placed them more-or-less in a straight line, outside the square, then peered out of the window, saying that he no longer wanted to play with them. The following week the play was repeated and again he was unable to sustain it once he had placed the animals. This activity continued for several weeks.

He excluded me from his activities in the earlier sessions but later vacillated between making use of me in the way that Winnicott (1971b) describes and excluding me. This was particularly obvious in a session towards the end of the term involving number work. Throughout the first term Osman was reluctant to read, to listen to stories, to draw or to write but was more responsive to work involving number, mainly counting. I presented him with a task that involved matching pictures of sets of objects to various numbers, all below five. I demonstrated the task to him, and we did the first page together. He was unable to manage the next page but rather than ask for my help he changed the task. He ignored my comment that he was no longer interested and began to circle sets quickly and impulsively. When I pointed out an obvious error he laughed boisterously.

Later in the session while playing with the animals he acknowledged some dependence. He was unsure which animals were farm animals and which were wild animals even though we had grouped them on previous occasions, and allowed me to help him distinguish them. He did not, however, verbalize his need but relied on holding up the animals so that I could see them.

I found Osman's withdrawn behaviour very difficult to cope with and am aware now that I tended to resort to being didactic. I was the one who introduced the idea of classifying the animals into farm and zoo animals and making Plasticene or paper 'food' for them. Both these initiatives became an established part of the animal play routine, not, I felt because Osman was being compliant and thought that this was what he had to do, but rather because he was going through the motions of playing, but was too frightened to have his own ideas. I felt that Osman's lack of spontaneity and his imitative behaviour, which were so striking during the first term, indicated that he had no sense of self as a valued individual and confirmed Father's comments at the first meeting that Osman was 'not his own person'.

Generally Osman's play with the animals seemed to lack any symbolic quality. It was as if he was using the animals to fill up the space, to fill up his own emptiness. I experienced his play as passive, unassertive and purpose-less. He would arrange the animals and then lose all motivation. I, too, felt a sense of helplessness and my uncertainty and lack of experience made me sometimes take refuge in being a teacher rather than trying to understand what I was learning.

During the second session, after initially expressing his feelings of inadequacy ('I can't . . . can't draw!') in response to my suggestion that he might like to draw, Osman produced three very strange, immature drawings; tiny foetus shaped figures enclosed in circles. He labelled them baby, mum, daddy. The drawings seemed to reflect a need to be contained and to be connected. They suggested the inability of baby, mum and daddy to communicate with each other. The circles in particular reminded me of a 'second skin' as described by Esther Bick (1968). At the next session I suggested that Osman might like to tell me a story about his drawing. He nodded enthusiastically, but then seemed at a loss. He found it extremely difficult but with a great deal of encouragement he dictated 'The baby and the mum and the daddy are sleeping. I like the dad and babies and mums. They are sleeping on the circle.'

This theme of unrelatedness was evident in the following session. To encourage Osman to find another means of communicating with me I began modelling in Plasticene. He decided I was making a pram. He seemed interested and helped me. At his instigation we made a baby. I helped Osman make the body and he made the arms and legs. They were quite out of proportion to the rest of the body and the baby would not fit into the pram. Osman appeared perturbed, and this made me speculate not only about his feelings about the baby, but also, again, about his difficulties in making use of his experience. He would presumably have had exposure to Plasticene as part of his nursery and infant school experience. My response to his being upset was to enlarge the pram to accommodate the baby and to ask whether he would like to make someone to push the pram. 'No' he said, 'it's all alone . . . no one's pushing it . . . it's sleeping.' He then turned his attention back to the animals.

Later in the session I suggested that the baby might no longer be asleep and would perhaps like to be taken for a walk to see the animals. I wondered who would take the baby for a walk, perhaps mummy and daddy. 'No', he said, 'only daddy.' Osman moved the pram towards the animals and then lifted out the baby. He seemed at a loss, so I commented that perhaps he was going to tell the baby the names of the animals. 'You don't talk to babies' was his immediate response. At this he put the baby in the pram and returned to the animals. He then began for the first time to play as though attaching some meaning to it. He began dropping the animals into the square made from the plastic fences and laughed loudly as they fell over. Then he covered the square with his head and his arms and when I asked what he was doing he said 'Magic.' This magic, which he repeated a number of times before telling me that he wanted to go, consisted of lifting up the square in one piece and leaving the animals inside. When we tidied away the animals Osman said he wanted to keep the pram. In the subsequent session the baby and pram were placed close to the animals, but ignored. At the end of the session he squashed them both and told me the pram had slipped.

The meaning of this play was not entirely clear to me although I felt that dropping the animals was in some way related to his own unconscious feelings aroused by the Plasticene baby. It made me think of Winnicott's idea of an infant 'infinitely falling' and not having an experience of being 'held'. Perhaps the magic made him feel omnipotent. I could not tell if the destruction of the baby and pram was because it no longer held any significance for him or whether the feelings aroused were so intense that he had to destroy the object that produced the feelings.

I was very touched by Osman's expression of feeling about the baby. The drawing and story of the foetus-shaped family and the model of the baby and pram suggested to me a baby who had not had his needs adequately met; his efforts had brought no response so he had given up hope. I felt that the parents illustrated this – that they represented a mother and father who were asleep and therefore unable to think about their baby; the baby was isolated and lacked attention. Osman's two comments 'He's all alone' and 'You don't talk to babies' seemed to confirm that all the baby could do was to sleep and show no interest in his surroundings. I was reminded of Bion's (1962a, 1962b) theory of the container and the contained and his reference to the role of a mother and her baby. His contention was that the baby's capacity to be curious and to think depends upon the baby's experience of being thought about by a mother in a way that makes him feel understood. The information given about Osman's early experience made me think that there were perhaps parallels between the feelings expressed in his drawings and model and what had been the reality of his early life.

Throughout the first term I found it hard to tolerate what I experienced as Osman's resistance to what I had to offer. I often felt distressed and the meaning of his behaviour eluded me. In retrospect I wonder whether my feelings were related not only to my own anxiety about how to interact with this withdrawn child with no basic skills but also to the feelings he was communicating. It did seem, however, that just being with Osman while he experienced his emptiness, my being able to tolerate our shared uncertainties, gave him a feeling of being contained. There was some indication of this in the final session, which had a restless and unsettled feel. He denied that there would be a break in the sessions but made a number of indirect references to it; he unravelled the sticky tape, he pretended the stapler was a telephone and he drew a dead fish on his hand.

SECOND TERM

Animal play: perseveration; difficulty in using imagination

Osman resumed his play with the animals during the second term, and in the early sessions it was as inhibited as it had been during the first term. A few weeks into the term Osman helped me build a train, alternating cylindrical and rectangular shaped bricks. When it was completed, I suggested that he might like to play with the animals as well. He got out the animals but then seemed to lose all motivation. When I suggested that they might like to go for a ride on the train he looked interested and placed them on the train but made no attempt to move it. He said he wanted to feed the animals as I had suggested in our earlier sessions. He cut out large irregular strips of sticky paper, far larger than any of the animals, coloured the reverse side of each strip in black, placed the strips in the train, and said 'I'm finished with the train and the animals.' His scissor control was good so the size of the strips could not be attributed to poor fine motor coordination. I wondered about the inappropriateness of the food in relation to the size of the animals.

In the following session Osman behaved in a similar way with the bricks and animals, but this time made an enclosure for the dog, another enclosure for the zoo animals, and a separate one for the farm animals. 'We must feed the animals', he said, giving me some paper and a pair of scissors, taking paper and scissors for himself and beginning to cut. I had no feeling of being involved but a strong sense of being controlled. Again, I was struck by the inappropriate feeding. 'The animals must be very hungry', I said. 'Make food' was his reply. 'I wonder what the animals are going to do now?' I asked, when all the food had been distributed. Osman looked at me in a perplexed way and a few minutes later muttered, 'I'm finished', which was then changed to 'I'm going to do magic.' Perhaps he interpreted my suggestion to mean that feeding the animals was not sufficient. He lifted the bricks surrounding the dog but to his utter consternation the dog wasn't there. It had got caught up with the bricks. For a moment Osman looked very frightened but then realized what had happened, rearranged the bricks and managed to perform the trick successfully.

I was taken aback by his response to the failure of his magic and sensed his helplessness and vulnerability as his feelings of omnipotence gave way to feelings of annihilation. As his sessions progressed, it became apparent that Osman identified closely with the dog. Separating the dog from the other animals, in this play that seemed preoccupied with separating off bits of himself, was a way of detaching himself from the chaotic feelings that seemed to overwhelm him; an attempt to keep a little of himself intact. For the magic not to work must indeed have been very frightening.

In most of the sessions that followed, when Osman played with the animals, there was a similar pattern of play. He isolated the animals, fed them, and more often than not did his magic with the dog. Sometimes he included me in this play, in an omnipotent way. At other times he ignored me. Osman's stereotyped play with the animals and the paucity of his verbal communication combined with almost no eye contact continued to communicate to me feelings of inadequacy and often made me feel anxious. In retrospect, I wonder whether my uncertainty led me to intervene too often. By intruding on Osman's space I think he experienced my comments as being unhelpful. Instead of reflecting back more of his feelings to him I tended sometimes to extend the play; at other times perhaps I did not enter sufficiently into the play with him. I was aware of feeling unsure of my role, and was concerned about my lack of interaction, but as the sessions continued, my observations of his behaviour made me feel that it was appropriate to 'hold' the situation in a Winnicottian sense – that it was appropriate to provide a setting in which he could regress.

Perhaps I was able to give Osman a sense of 'being held' because there was a subtle change in the animal play just before the end of term. In the penultimate session he became very absorbed in his play, spending most of the session slowly and carefully building a complicated connected structure for the animals. He seemed almost lost in a dream, unaware of my presence at times, but once or twice he acknowledged my presence by looking at me. 'There must be place for the food' was the only comment he made, as he manipulated the bricks to make an enclosure solely for the food. When he was satisfied that all the animals were placed in the way he wanted them, he said to me 'I'll feed them just now' and got up from the carpet. In the final session he played in the same preoccupied way and although he hardly communicated with me, he seemed to take my presence for granted. At one point, as a door banged loudly he looked up and asked me about the noise, and then returned to his play, forgetting me. When he had finished I asked if he would like to tell me a story about them. He nodded, but found the task almost impossible and could only manage a few disjointed sentences.

The animals having to wait for their food suggested that Osman was beginning to build up a feeling of continuity about himself, to take inside himself a mirror image of 'going-on-being'. He was beginning to internalize sufficient good mothering to enable him to delay gratification. There was a feeling in these two sessions of Osman having reached the first stage outlined in Winnicott's (1971a, 1971b) theory of the development of play, namely playing alone in the presence of someone. According to Winnicott, being able to play implies trust – the child plays because he can rely on an adult being available when remembered after being forgotten. It seemed that Osman was beginning to trust me a little.

The three little pigs: difficulty with symbolic thinking

I did not suggest that Osman read to me during this term and did very little educational work with him, apart from some work on concept formation – abstraction such as size and shape – work on number bonds to 10s, and simple sets. Osman was unable to cope with simple classification tasks such as sorting for both size and shape, and this made me realize how restricted his capacity for abstract thinking was. In retrospect, I am aware that the work I did was largely irrelevant. Osman was too anxious to learn and I did not make sufficient allowances for his state of mind.

His difficulty in symbolic thinking became apparent when I read stories to him. As I have indicated, during the first term he was extremely resistant to listening to stories. Early in the second term we looked through a storybook and Osman seemed interested in the illustrations accompanying *The Three Little Pigs*. He sat quietly and listened as I started reading, but when I reached the part where the wolf wants to eat one of the little pigs he interrupted with 'My daddy doesn't eat pig and I don't eat pig.' A few minutes later he said that he wanted to go. It seemed as if father not eating the pork got in the way of his listening to the story; something other than the words themselves were affecting his understanding. I wondered about his capacity for symbol formation because his response seemed to suggest that he had difficulty with the symbol equation. According to Dorothy Davidson (1988) the story illustrates the precarious character of early boundaries and the fragile sense of identity. It seemed as if the symbol was the dreaded object, and Osman identified with the object because he did not know that his self was separate from other people. He had no effective basis for sublimation (Weininger, 1989).

The following week Osman had forgotten the story completely, suggesting that because he felt that there was no space inside him to safely hold fearful thoughts, he was unable to retain them. I read it again but he had a bemused expression on his face and the only comment he made was that he did not eat pig. At the next session he said that he didn't want to hear the story, but acknowledged that he found it frightening. In retrospect, I realize that instead of dealing with his anxiety I offered reassurance by saying that he was not ready to hear about the wolf.

I began the following session by telling him the story in simplified form, omitting, at this and all subsequent sessions, all references to the tricks the wolf used to get the third pig out of the house, and emphasizing how clever the third little pig was. Osman found it extremely hard to cope with the wolf's destruction – he shuffled about in his chair, and once or twice interrupted to tell me he could see his daddy's car, which was in fact visible from where we were sitting. When we reached the end of the story I suggested he draw a picture of the wolf and this he did with a lot of coaxing. I drew a pot of water under the wolf and Osman tentatively drew some flames. He was very quiet and as soon as he had finished asked to do something else. He was obviously still experiencing so much anxiety, because of his hostile and persecutory feelings, that he needed to escape to counteract his fear of being overwhelmed. At the end of the session to my surprise, he asked for the story again. He listened intently at first, but then kept on wanting to turn over the pages and when we got to the end of the story he turned over as if to reassure himself that it was the end of the wolf.

Osman did not return to the story for a while. He missed a number of sessions due to half term and illness, but three sessions later he asked me to read him the story. His interest was more sustained but he appeared confused when we discussed the sequence of events. The repetition of this story from time to time over the next year in the presence of a reliable adult enabled Osman, I felt, to begin to trust and to be less overwhelmed by his feelings of being devoured. Bettelheim (1976) in *The Uses of Enchantment* wrote that fairy stories do not refer to the outer world but to inner processes taking place in the child. He saw the wolf in the story as a projection of a child's badness: a child's wish to devour and facing the consequences of a possible similar attack on himself. Osman's reaction to the story suggested a difficulty in symbolic thinking, that he became overwhelmed by his phantasies about father eating pork and that his phantasies provided a barrier that prevented the meaning of words being taken in by him.

THIRD TERM

A secure base

During the third term there was a sense of the continuity of sessions being remembered. As the term progressed it became evident that Osman was feeling more secure in his relationship with me, although there were times when he kept me at arms length and was very controlling. His thinking became a little less inhibited, but I was struck by his disordered thought and language processes. He was interested in the educational materials that I brought to the sessions, and his play with the animals became more elaborated, with some indications of aggressive feelings. He began to show some curiosity about me, and also to make links for himself between home, school and his sessions at the clinic. In terms of Bowlby's (1969) theory of attachment behaviour, he seemed to be beginning to develop a secure base from which he could explore the world around him. According to Bowlby, separation from the mother coincides with exploration of the environment, and in this way the toddler begins to experience himself as an individual.

There were indications of curiosity, perhaps greed for new experiences as early as the second session of the term. He rushed ahead of me to the room and immediately started looking through his box. 'You are in a hurry today', I commented. 'I'm going to play with the animals', he said, but just then caught sight of something on the shelf. 'What's that?' he asked. I explained that it was a word game (a simple phonics game) and that he might like to play the game later. 'I want to play with it now.' I gave him a choice and he chose the game, enjoying it and accepting my help with words he found difficult.

He was interested in new materials but there was also a willingness to work with familiar materials in different ways. Osman enjoyed using the Unifix cubes, but his main interest centred on building up towers of numbers and making staircases of 1 to 10. I was aware of the importance of this to him; building up the cubes seemed to suggest building up a sense of himself. After a few weeks of this repetitive way of working I presented him with groups of six Unifix cubes and we set about finding different ways of making six. I demonstrated the task to him (e.g. $4 + 2$) but he found it difficult and frequently wanted to repeat the same pattern. I sensed a more relaxed attitude in the way he accepted my help, and when I offered praise on completion of the task I was aware of his feelings of satisfaction. Maths is about relationships and Osman's difficulty with this task suggested how hard it was for him to think about separation.

Towards the end of the term, because of my concern about his poor language skills, I gave him the British Picture Vocabulary Scale Test. Osman's response to this task demonstrated how confident he was becoming in tackling an unfamiliar task. He helped me set up the booklet, and showed pleasure when he recognized pictures relating to words, saying 'It's easy'. When recognition was difficult he did not seem to be overwhelmed: 'I don't know that'. I was particularly interested in his response to the word 'pair'. 'A pair of shoes?' he asked, but instead of choosing the pair of shoes, he chose a single shoe. Separation in any form was a difficult concept to contend with.

Emergent thinking

Towards the middle of the term I began reading Osman a story titled *Time to Get Out of the Bath, Shirley* by John Burningham. He made no comment, but the following week when we returned to the story, he turned to me, and said, in a slightly surprised tone 'She doesn't listen'. When we turned the page he asked 'Is she having a dream?' 'What do you think?' was my response. He was silent for a moment and then said 'Why she's going down the water? ... she's going to go under.' I reflected his anxiety back to him and then went on to explain about bathroom pipes.

Mirroring; confusion

In one of the sessions Osman chose *The Dog and the Bone* from the storybook. I told him the story, using the illustrations, but it seemed beyond his comprehension; he appeared to have no understanding of mirror reflections. He returned to the story the following week, but repetition did not increase his understanding. 'I wonder who you see when you look in the mirror?' I asked. 'Daddy.' I brought a mirror to the next session and when he looked in it he smiled, saying 'It's Osman.' 'It is, it's Osman smiling', I confirmed. It was from this period that I began to feel that Osman was beginning to discover himself, but discovery was not untroubled. The precariousness of his concept of oneness was evident a few months later when he was doing some simple thinking-skill tasks, which required him to answer yes or no to questions. 'Can you see yourself in the mirror?' 'No' he replied. 'What can you see?' I asked. 'Nothing.'

In the light of Winnicott's paper on mirroring (in Winnicott, 1971b), Osman's responses made me question again his early experience, and whether he had had sufficient messages of confirmation that he was Osman. Winnicott, in this paper, wrote that when the baby looks at the mother's face and does not get back what he is giving, he does not see himself. One of the consequences of this is that the baby's own creative capacity begins to atrophy and he looks for other ways of getting something of himself back from the environment. I wondered if Osman was a baby who was not responded to and at an early age withdrew from a threat of chaos.

Angry feelings

In parallel with Osman's emergent thinking and capacity for learning educationally in the narrow sense, he was also able to play more aggressively. This was demonstrated when I added a crocodile to the animals that were already in his box. In his animal play he built a separate enclosure for the hippo and for the crocodile, but then placed the crocodile next to the hippo. It transpired that the crocodile was going to eat the hippo, but then Osman changed his mind. I felt as if his anxieties about the crocodile and hippo could not be tolerated, so they had to be denied. Later in the session I suggested that he might like to tell me a story about the crocodile and the hippo. He appeared willing, but found it difficult. He was quiet for a few moments and then said 'Giraffe.' 'Is there going to be a giraffe in the story?' 'Panda' was his reply. It seemed safer to think of less threatening animals.

With help he began the story. 'He's going to eat the hippo and all the food . . . I think frogs live in zoos.' I reflected back to him how hard it was to think of a story and then asked why the crocodile was going to eat the hippo. 'Because the hippo's afraid of the croc . . . the croc's going to be dead one day . . . because he ate the hippo.' Osman seemed to be grappling with the fear of his own wish to bite as well as fear of being bitten. His hostility, in his phantasy, led to destruction, the death of the crocodile. I compared the crocodile to the wolf in the story of the *The Three Little Pigs* and as the play continued I was left with the impression that Osman worked out some of his feelings about aggression and fear of retaliation without any intervention from me. It seemed as if he felt secure enough to explore some of his feelings of oral aggression without being completely overwhelmed by persecutory phantasies resulting from his projective identification.

FOURTH TERM

More reading; making connections; risking more thinking

During the fourth term Osman's behaviour suggested he was more in touch with his feelings. He was more animated, more alert and more communicative, and there were changes in the manner of his play. He chose to play with the animals less often, and when he did, the play was more imaginative and less stereotyped. He began, too, to use Plasticene more imaginatively. At times he involved me in his play in a way that suggested that he had reached the first stage of mutual play, as described by Winnicott (1971a, 1971b). He continued to enjoy simple repetitive number work but I felt his understanding of number was very limited. He was able to read mechanically, relying mainly on word recognition. He became less resistant to reading books, and began to attach some meaning to the stories he read.

A few weeks into the fourth term Osman read a story about a cat that becomes fatter and fatter, hides in a cupboard, and is later found with a litter of kittens. At the end of the story he was able to tell me that the kittens came 'from the mummy's tummy'. He seemed entranced by the picture of the big fluffy cat. 'She's round' he said softly, and gently traced her outline with his fingers, in a way that seemed to me to suggest that he had lost something. I was reminded of this a few months later when he drew a tummy. (My tummy had rumbled rather loudly and when Osman said that it was 'because of all the things inside' I suggested he drew a tummy.) He drew something reminiscent of a Christmas tree. 'That's the skeletal' and then added a figure enclosed in a circle. This, he said, was the baby in my tummy. 'Oh, I've got a baby in my tummy?' He nodded. 'Is there a baby in your tummy too?' Osman categorically denied this. 'I'm a boy, boys don't have babies in their tummies, only ladies do.' 'All ladies?' I asked. 'Yes.' 'Does mummy have a baby in her tummy?'. 'Yes.' 'I wonder when it's going to come out of her tummy?' 'When it's big.' I felt touched by this. I felt as if Osman wanted to be a baby again – a baby in my tummy. It was as if he was letting me know that his emergent self did not like what he saw of the world around him, and wanted to go back into the womb.

I thought about his responses in relation to Melanie Klein's theory of the epistemological instinct (Klein, 1931). She said that the mother's body 'represents in the unconscious the treasure house of everything desirable.' The fat, round cat and my tummy seemed to be associated with feelings of security perhaps an idealized mother and this seemed in direct contrast with the conscious feelings that Osman had about his own mother's body. Mother, in reality, smoked heavily and this preoccupied Osman a great deal – many of his drawings contained smoke, sometimes fire, and he once voiced his fears that his mother might die from smoking too much.

A few sessions after he had read the story about the cat, Osman started reading the fable about the ants and the grasshopper. He misread grasshopper as 'grasshooper', and laughed as he corrected his mistake. 'I wonder why he's called a grasshopper?' I asked. 'I can't think' he replied. I reflected back to him that we all find it hard to think sometimes. Osman seemed reluctant to continue reading, and instead of keeping him on task I went along with him. This resulted in him taking over the session. He moved from one activity to another, avoiding everything, controlling everything. I tried to engage him in some imaginative play but he turned away from me. He was able to show me some of his feelings of despair – his feeling that a good internal object was no longer available to him. 'I'm a bit tired.... ! think I'm finished ... ! can't play... It's too long in the clinic.'

I found this session very upsetting and in thinking about the meaning of Osman's communication I understood how much I had let him down; I understood that he needed to keep me under control because I left him sensing that his negative feelings could not be tolerated, when I had allowed him to abandon the reading activity. I began the next session by suggesting that we should read the story again. When Osman got to the second sentence and read 'The little ants were hard at work' I intervened. I said that we had not managed to do any work the previous week and that I felt sad because things seemed to have gone wrong and I had not been able to help him. He said 'Yes' very quietly, and looked at me in a way that suggested he felt that I understood him. When he turned over the page and read 'The grasshopper was not hard at work' I said that last week he had reminded me of a grasshopper, hopping around from one thing to another, and not being able to do any work. He laughed gently and nodded, and went on to finish the story.

Osman's understanding of the story was minimal, but he seemed to understand something of greater importance. By talking to him about the events of the previous session I think that I might have helped him perceive that I was able to understand his negative feelings and that he could trust me. I became aware of this later in the session when he chose to play with the animals and in his play was able to show his more aggressive feelings. He emptied all the animals out of the packet, but chose only to play with the crocodile and Mr and Mrs Lion. 'I'm going to fight them' he said, as the lion and the crocodile attacked each other, the lion seeming to get slightly the upper hand. Then Mrs Lion joined in the attack on the crocodile. 'Mrs Lion is fighting the crocodile' I remarked. 'She's strong', replied Osman, suggesting to me that he felt that I was strong enough to bear his aggressive feelings.

Osman read some stories with obvious pleasure and rudimentary understanding, but in his response to other stories there was still evidence of his confused and uncertain inner world. Towards the end of the term he began reading a story about a hamster in a classroom. When he got to the part where the hamster escapes from his cage he stopped reading, and was reluctant to continue. 'I've got a headache', he said. 'I've got a feeling.' 'What kind of feeling?' I asked. 'I've got a feeling ... can you tell me about it?' This poignant reply reminded me of Bion's (1962a, 1962b) reference to 'nameless dread'. I reflected back to Osman how hard it was for him to think of the hamster running away and possibly getting lost, and went on to suggest we read the story together and he managed to tolerate listening to it.

Osman continued to read stories during the next two terms and there was evidence that he was beginning to understand the sequence of events. In one story he read, some animals thought that a water hose was a snake. He was unable to predict this for himself as he read the story but when the pictures in the book clarified this he laughed loudly. 'That's not a snake. It's a water-hose.' At the end of the story he laughed again: 'Silly animals ... It was the water.'

Ghosts

The first reference to ghosts came during a session when I took Osman to the cloak-room to wash his hands after the use of some Plasticene. He was unable to move past the door and became rooted to the spot. 'I can't . . . ! frightened' was all he could say. He regained his composure once we returned to our room but could offer no explanation until the next session when he was able to tell me that he had been frightened by a ghost. He was unable to elaborate, but drew a strange picture with disparate items including himself with a spinning wheel in his head. I felt disturbed by the drawing, which had a sexual feel about it. His story suggested some gender confusion and was about a little ghost 'that can only go backwards and a big ghost that can go backwards and forwards.'

He continued, 'The big ghost goes far, far away. The fat man has a fat chest because he ate a lot and there is smoke. He's a man lady because he's wearing a dress.' The figure of himself suggested a feeling of powerlessness, being controlled by a spinning wheel.

FIFTH TERM

Mutual play; pleasure in learning

What came across forcibly during the fifth term's work with Osman was a sense of how far he had moved since the beginning of his educational psychotherapy sessions. When I started working with him he was withdrawn, with a very confused picture of himself. He had, to borrow A. A. Milne's phrase, 'hardly begun'. By the fifth term there was a sense of a more integrated self and I felt as if there was the beginning of a relationship that was being consolidated in each new session. Generally, he was eager to show me that he could do things 'by himself' and he took pleasure in his achievements. In many respects he reminded me of a much younger child who was just starting school. There was a change in the way Osman interacted with me, and this was particularly evident when we played word card games and number games, which were a prominent feature of the term's work. In playing these games there was evidence of the second stage of mutual play, described by Winnicott (1971a, 1971b). Osman was playing with me – we were playing together in a relationship.

I can best illustrate Osman's spontaneity and change in attitude by referring to some of the work that we did relating to number. I reintroduced a game with addition bonds to 20, to which Osman had previously not been very responsive. 'Hey it's not the same', he said, pointing to the die, which had numbers instead of dots. 'It's a different die. How clever of you to remember after such a long time!' Osman looked pleased with himself at this praise. When I asked whether he would like to play the game he joined in enthusiastically. 'I don't believe it', he said in a mock affronted tone of voice when he landed on a square he had already covered. At one point, when he noticed that I was further along the board than he was, he said, 'I'm only here and you're there.' He was enormously pleased by the application of his own skills when he won.

We were to play this game and other board games, and card games, many times. Osman always played enthusiastically, wholly engrossed in the game. He often laughed happily and enjoyed beating me, which I surreptitiously allowed him to do quite often. There were times when he coped well with the number bonds, spontaneously remembering some of them, but at other times he needed to go back to basics, counting out numbers rather than counting on. However, I was more than once surprised at his capacity to anticipate where he would need to land on a square in order to beat me.

Winning delighted Osman because it affirmed his ability. He would often tell me that I had not won because I did not know how to play. Before one of the termly parental meetings, I discussed with Osman what he would like me to tell his parents. 'Tell them I win ... Because I'm good.' (The consultant psychiatrist did not wish Osman to attend family meetings.) Winning at games was, for Osman, some sort of proof that he could manage for himself. He would often tell his father, excitedly, at the end of the session that he had beaten me. Father found it difficult to believe that his son could win without cheating! This made me question whether Osman expected me to cheat. Was that the reason I did not know how to play the game?

I used the number games to teach Osman the concepts of 'more than' and 'less than'. One of the games involved large numbers of different coloured counters, so I suggested at the end of a game that we form two matching rows of counters, to see who had more. He was able to see at a glance that he had more counters but even with one-to-one correspondence he was unable to understand that he had four more. I thought about the subtlety of the words 'more' and 'less' and how difficult it must be for Osman who had not had enough experience to understand these concepts. I varied the ways in which I tried to teach him these concepts but with little success. Osman enjoyed comparing numbers when we played games and often spontaneously suggested we count to see who had more counters. He became able mechanically to produce the correct answer by comparing rows or columns, but real understanding eluded him. During these activities I realized that the concepts of 'more' or 'less' must be inordinately difficult to master for a child who took so long to struggle to understand the concept of one or oneness. In our activities to learn 'more' and 'less' I recalled Winnicott's paper 'Sum I Am' published posthumously (1986).

I was reminded of his difficulty with this concept in a later session, when he was reading a story in which one of the characters ate 10 sandwiches at a party. 'Ten sandwiches', he commented in amazement, then laughed. 'I don't like him ... He's too fat, greedy. Later I'm going to play the number game.' This seemed to suggest that for Osman there was no point in being greedy, he would not get what he wanted. Perhaps the reference to the game was a reassurance that he was going to get something that would give him pleasure.

There were indications during this term of his ability to use numbers in the real world. In one session he was reading a story in which a boy turned six and received a badge with six on it. Osman told me he had got a badge when he was nine. 'I passed six, and I passed seven, and I passed eight, and when I pass nine, I'll be 10.' This was the first indication I had of his concept of time and a belief that he had a future.

FINAL TERM

Separations and ending

Over the period of time that I worked with Osman he became more able to tolerate separations although in this, as in all other aspects of his functioning, there was no clear-cut progression. In the early stages he used the defences of shutting off and forgetting. When I talked about impending breaks he could not listen and when he resumed sessions he seemed to have forgotten everything that had happened previously.

In the latter part of the first year there were indications that the sessions were becoming more important to him, and that he was beginning to trust me. In the final session of the second term he spent a lot of time folding pieces of paper and stapling, gluing and sellotaping them together, as if symbolically enfolding both of us as a way of holding the memory of the session together. He used up all the staples and told me to get some more, indicating that he could rely on me to be there after the break to fill up the emptiness perhaps.

Later on, before a half-term break, he was more able to express feelings directly. He asked me to write not only his name but also his telephone number on a drawing and, when I reflected back his need to maintain contact and that I would be thinking of him, he nodded and said 'Wednesday' – the day of our sessions. Sometimes he projected his feelings of abandonment onto me when I discussed breaks. 'My dad's going in the plane and my mum. You won't see me. I'll be in Turkey.'

At the end of the first year we made a calendar for him to take home because he was having tremendous difficulty understanding the sequence of events. He asked me to write on it 'When Merkel and Osman won't be able to see each other.' At the end of the session when I took him back to father, he waved it excitedly, saying, 'Merkel made me a letter when she's not coming.' I realized afterwards how important it was for him to have some concrete evidence of the separation. The calendar was a reminder of my existence for this boy whose ego, I felt, was still so frail. The incongruity between his apparent gaiety and what the calendar represented made me aware of how much he was still denying painful feelings.

By the beginning of the second year his behaviour suggested that he was building up an internal working model of a reliable mother figure. When I reminded him about the impending half-term break during the fourth term he turned and asked 'Whose bed?' referring to the couch in the room. He nodded in agreement when I wondered whether he thought it was my bed. Keeping me in the room would ensure my continued existence despite the separation.

On another occasion I was reminded of Winnicott's idea of children having a sense of 'going-on-being' when Osman unconsciously used a symbol to express his feelings about the Christmas break. He was doing a simple sequencing task, arranging pictures to tell a story about a kite stuck in a tree. Instead of placing the cards in semantic order he chose to focus on connecting the cards in terms of the string attached to the kite. I felt this indicated his need for continuity and reminded me of an umbilical cord.

Osman's anxiety about thinking was demonstrated just before a break. We had made another calendar the previous week, which he had taken home, but in this session he seemed to have forgotten all about it. He looked distressed when I asked about the calendar and said, 'I can't think'. His anxiety appeared to have destroyed his capacity to know about the calendar. I acknowledged how difficult it was for him to think when he was upset. 'I've got it', he said after a few moments in a quiet voice.

By the fifth term there was recognition of me as a separate person. When he returned to his sessions after a break he openly expressed curiosity about me. 'Do you live in a house?' 'Do you live with your daddy?' He was able to show his ambivalence when I reminded him about a break by making some Plasticene 'food'; mine was burnt.

Changes

During the final term Osman was able to show how much he was beginning to be able to use the sessions to work out his confused and empty internal world. There were many references to power, both in his animal play and in his drawings. He seemed to be exploring his internal confusion about projection and introjection of feelings. His drawings suggested a preoccupation with power and feelings of tremendous aggression towards father. Many of the drawings were about policemen and robbers. The policeman was always smaller than the robber and it seemed as if Osman was the policeman and father the robber. Although both his animal play and drawings reflected confusion and anxiety there was also evidence of ego functioning at a more mature level. He continued to take pleasure in the games we played and to enjoy reading as well as new activities such as finger painting.

On one level, Osman's major preoccupation during the final term was the fact that he was going to move schools and stop his sessions with me that term. A decision was not made until the final week of term regarding Osman's future placement and his parents were understandably anxious about what would happen to him. It was obvious that the parents' anxieties and their conversations in Osman's presence were creating difficulties for him and making him feel insecure. He often resorted to omnipotence as a way of coping with his anxiety and confusion. He rubbished the school he attended but his anxiety was evident when, after he had read me a story about secret wishes, he admitted that he wished his new school 'would be nice'.

The child psychiatrist felt that Osman was ready for child psychotherapy, so early in the term I began preparing him for the fact that he would no longer be working with me after the summer holidays but with an unknown psychotherapist. His initial response was denial. He was glad, he said. When I reflected this back to him he said with a placatory smile 'OK I'm sad.' At the end of this session he did his 'magic'.

As the term progressed, Osman struggled to cope with his feelings about the ending, vacillating between acceptance and denial. After half-term there was a sense of Osman really registering that there would be an ending. We had been sitting on the carpet playing a card game, which he won and enjoyed winning. I got up and went back to the table but Osman, for the first time ever, went to sit on one of the large chairs in the corner of the room, an indication, perhaps, of his spontaneous functioning, of 'being himself'. It seemed as if he was exploring the room, exploring what he knew he was going to lose. He looked around and then said 'That's not your bed.'

The next session there was direct reference to his feelings. He asked me how to spell a word while he was labelling his drawing and remarked 'When someone's 11 they know how to do things.' I commented that he seemed to be ready to think about growing up and being able to manage when he was 11. At the end of the session as we counted the number of weeks left on his calendar I felt he was recognizing his need to be dependent as he said 'Am I going to see someone else? I don't want to. I want to see you.'

When there were a few sessions left I used the unifix cubes to represent them. Osman's response to this was to join about 80 cubes together. 'I'm going to do it long', indicating his wish to prolong the time we had left. His reluctance to end the session and the fact that he put the cubes away in a different way from usual also showed me his realization that there had to be an ending. During the next session he asked me whether I would be seeing someone else. I acknowledged his sadness and my own and again told him, as I had been doing throughout the term that I would think about him. He gave me a funny, surprised smile and a few moments later said 'It's going to be Sports Day next Friday.' 'It sounds like you want to think about something different', I said. 'You can take the animals and bricks home . . . keep them there', he mumbled.

I approached the final session with trepidation because I knew it would be difficult for both of us. Osman nodded solemnly when I told him it was the last time we would be working together. The session had a quiet feeling about it, but somehow his choice of activities made it all right. He talked to me as he glued and stapled paper together. 'It's going to be my last day in school', a recognition that both school and clinic sessions were ending. 'I'm putting lots of Sellotape so I can cut it out . . . [he cut off a bit] . . . It's a sailor's hat. Look at this.' I felt as if he had succeeded not only in sticking the sessions together, but was taking on board that he was leaving, sailing away. 'I'm going to do the animals now.' He said, as he went to sit on the carpet. He had ignored the animals for a long time but today they were obviously important. His mood changed to one of preoccupation as he used the bricks to build enclosures for the animals. Unlike all his previous animal play he did not roof in the dog: He fed all the animals except the dog. I felt that he was telling me that the dog was feeling safer and could manage on his own without being fed in this session.

On our return to the waiting room we said goodbye and, as I spoke to his father Osman interrupted me, saying, 'I'm not coming to this clinic any more. I don't like it.' Despite this final denial I felt confident that he had internalized something 'good enough' from his sessions.

COMMENTARY ON 'CASE STUDY OF OSMAN'

The story of the work with Osman illustrates a number of ways in which the educational psychotherapist understands the relationship between the child's emotional development and his/her ability to learn.

There is a certain amount of information about Osman's developmental history and family background. The therapist comments that the clinic notes 'do not provide a great deal of information'. This is a feeling that often takes hold of us when learning about something or someone new. There is a sense that if only we had enough information the learning process would become easier.

When working as an educational psychotherapist, it is useful to have some idea of what has happened to the child in the past, so that a hypothesis can be made about the factors that may have affected his/her ability to learn. In this case, a restricted social life and the competing demands, for his mother, of work and home are suggested as contributory elements and seem to have been compounded by the 'quite hopeless' childcare arrangements that his parents had had to make for him.

Osman's own response is summed up in a description of him as a 'good' baby, despite the fact that he would not breast feed and refused solids when they were first offered at two to three months. He has acquired the developmental skills of walking and toilet training at appropriate times but there is a concern on the part of people outside the family about his language development. Although he has responded to speech therapy, he has found it difficult to transfer this new learning to the school context. The speech therapist has noted, with concern, Osman's difficulty in separating from his father when he has come for sessions.

It is this latter point that the therapist has particularly in mind when she meets him for the first time. However, she needs to set aside her thoughts about his background and early history in order to be receptive to what the child brings to the session. She makes careful note of his appearance and observes the way he responds to her, to the tasks she offers him and to the situation of being in an unfamiliar learning environment. She is able to note the 'glimmer of interest' that gives her the opportunity to separate Osman and his father in a way that is manageable for both of them. She is able to link her own feelings of anxiety and inadequacy with feelings that Osman might be experiencing.

The psychotherapist is also alert to the ways in which Osman defends himself against his feelings of anxiety and inadequacy. She refers to his desire to be in control rather than allowing the possibility of not knowing. He frequently repeats the same action (filling up the Connect frame with counters) and thus avoids the need to relate to the psychotherapist or to remember what has happened in the past and try to apply that experience to a new one. She is also aware of her own need, at times, to defend herself against the feeling of rejection she experiences when working with Osman and suggests that at times like these she found herself becoming didactic.

The work that Osman produces is not merely used as an example of what he can do. It also becomes a valuable opportunity to understand more of the way in which he sees himself in relation to the outside world. He feels cut off from those closest to him, and unable to communicate with them. The educational psychotherapist needs to work sensitively with this feeling to try and introduce the possibility that these feelings can be contained. She begins to make a Plasticene model the following week and Osman identifies this as a pram. There then begins an interaction between them, which allows him to make a link between this and the animals he had previously used. This is a tentative beginning of play and creativity.

At this point, the educational psychotherapist has various items of knowledge about Osman and is able to review her hypothesis about the origin of his learning difficulties. She brings together all the aspects of her knowledge of him, and draws on psychoanalytic theory to develop her thinking about him and to understand the parallels between the feelings expressed in his drawing and model, and the reality of his own early experience. This enables her to be aware of the intense anxiety surrounding any learning task and to recognize that all the noneducational activities they do can contribute to the development of his capacity to think symbolically and to interact with a person or a task.

As she introduces stories into their work together, the educational psychotherapist has, again, to be aware of the way in which a story can be a metaphorical representation of aspects of the child's experience. In this way, it can either provide a possible solution to some of the child's problems or can introduce thoughts that the child is not yet ready to deal with. When she reads the story of *The Three Little Pigs*, Osman is made so anxious by the aggressive feelings of the wolf that he finds it intolerable and wants to withdraw from the session. She found that he dealt with this anxiety by apparently 'forgetting' the story between one week and the next and she was able to adapt the story and make it manageable for him.

The insights gained by the educational psychotherapist and by the child into his situation, are enhanced by the careful boundaries set out by her. The same room is used at a regular time, and the child begins to understand that the time is for him to use and that the educational psychotherapist can offer a 'secure base'. The sense of loss surrounding the breaks in the work together can be thought about and there is the possibility that therapist and child can hold each other in mind when they are not together. The box used by the therapist to introduce learning and play materials and in which these are kept for the child also symbolizes the 'containing' space that she provides and her capacity to keep both the child and the things he has produced safe.

The educational psychotherapist maintains good contact with the school throughout the work. Not surprisingly, despite being experienced and caring, his class teacher initially struggles to cope with Osman. Over time she does notice positive changes in him but it is common to see a time lag between progress in the therapy room and in school. It seems unlikely that in a large group Osman would make a bid for attention from the teacher or ask for help. The challenge would be to keep him connected to her, to give him words for his experiences and to gauge precisely how much pressure he could manage. He finds it overwhelmingly painful to face his limitations and – because of his limited capacity for symbolization so that the content and processes in learning are potentially frightening – new educational challenges in class would need to be very sensitively introduced.

Osman struggles socially in class and might benefit from close monitoring of relationships with other children as well as careful preparation for meeting unfamiliar adults such as supply teachers. His teacher might also consider whether she has a role in relation to his parents in supporting their understanding of his emotional developmental level. Guidance about appropriate reading material and activities at home might be helpful to them.

The educational psychotherapist shares with us the development of this child's capacity to learn and her pleasure at his doing so. But there are other feelings around working with a child and she also experiences some of these. Her awareness of the child and his needs makes it difficult to be sanguine about the less aware responses of some of the other adults who engage with him. It is difficult not to feel a sense of rivalry with parents or other professionals. It is also difficult to end the work knowing that there is much more for the child to learn and that the opportunity he needs may not be there.

3 Initial Assessment of Emotional Factors Contributing to a Child's Learning Difficulties

INTRODUCTION

Osman's educational psychotherapist gives a moving account of the first sessions with him where she begins to gain a picture of a fragile, frightened child with few basic skills and little sense of agency. Despite her initial feelings of anxiety and inadequacy when faced with his withdrawn and uncommunicative behaviour, she sees that she might offer something of value to him in her role as educational psychotherapist. Consequently she sets out to provide an environment where he ultimately feels safe enough to risk thinking and feeling.

In the normal way of things educational psychotherapists offer a dedicated few sessions for assessment of a child's suitability for the intervention before ongoing work is offered. At the end of this period they meet with the family and visit the school to feed back their views about continuing the work.

Osman, despite significant cognitive and emotional limitations, demonstrated a capacity to make use of important aspects of an educational psychotherapy approach. We saw first of all that he responded to the 'containment' offered. That is, his awareness of an adult who could think about and make sense of his responses made him feel safe. He was able to remain in the room without his father present and to engage, rudimentarily, in activities with his therapist. When faced with a task he quickly revealed both his anxiety and his attempts to deal with it. He clearly benefited from a fairly structured approach, finding it easier to interact indirectly with the adult with an activity serving as a 'meeting point' between them. It became apparent that he had missed out on important early emotional experiences of learning within a relationship and would benefit from a therapy that mimicked this.

As a general rule the children best suited to an educational psychotherapy approach tend to be those who:

- underachieve academically for emotional reasons;
- are defended and fragile – and respond well to structure;
- prefer an indirect approach to exploring personal issues;
- need to regulate proximity to the teacher;
- harbour family secrets or 'unspeakable' thoughts;

- can engage in a task or activity;
- are 'anxiously attached' to their carers.

Some of the materials and approaches described in this chapter will be familiar to specialist teachers. An educational psychotherapy assessment, however, is informed by theoretical concepts drawn mainly from psychoanalysis and there is a greater emphasis on identifying unconscious factors influencing a child's academic achievement. Questions are posed not only about what a child knows or can or cannot do but also what phantasies underlie the learning difficulty and what the teacher may represent for that child. Teachers are highly skilled at working with the conscious, more accessible side of pupils but also benefit from understanding the nature of a child's relationships and the very particular unconscious meaning that curriculum content and processes may have for the child. The concepts and some of the strategies described will therefore have relevance to teachers in any setting.

In this chapter we first consider some factors in setting the scene for the assessment and meeting the child. We then give a flavour of the kind of information the educational psychotherapist will be seeking and some of the techniques and materials she uses to elicit it. The nature of a child's attachment is considered. Finally we describe the standard assessment procedure.

Many of the ideas described are elaborated in Chapter 7.

MEETING THE CHILD

Assessing the child is an exciting and significant process. No two children respond in quite the same way and, despite detailed referral information, there can be surprising new insights into children's views of the world and their relationships to people or educational challenges. There is sometimes a danger that referral information may preoccupy educational psychotherapists, who must set aside pre-existing expectations and assumptions so that they can make a fresh observation. In class children have an opportunity to be seen differently when their teacher changes – particularly if the teacher can look beyond the children's habitual behaviour and be aware of more hidden aspects of their personalities.

Because of the heightened sense of anxiety and also hopefulness that children bring to a new relationship, the opportunity to observe their responses is maximized in these early sessions and the therapist must assume that everything that the child does or says may be significant. The impact of being in a testing situation alone with an unfamiliar adult can be profound for some vulnerable children. We saw the effect of anxiety on Osman when he was unable to think or find words. In contrast, another child revealed his hopefulness about finding a receptive adult by immediately producing a story that revealed his anxieties about his destructiveness. He called it 'The boy who spoilt everything and broke up the world.'

Teachers or educational psychotherapists meeting a child for the first time will also be bringing views and feelings arising from their own history and circumstances.

Awareness of this supports their capacity to see the child clearly and objectively. The studies show how they, too, may struggle with anxiety as they make the transition from experienced teacher to trainee educational psychotherapist. Managing a temporary sense of uncertainty, ignorance and feelings of being deskilled can be a useful reminder of the pupil's experience and of the enormous difficulty for insecure children of acknowledging helplessness.

Before discussing what educational psychotherapists want to know about children it may be useful to consider what they may want children to know about them. They hope that children will experience them as receptive individuals who are interested in them without being intrusive or 'investigative' – individuals who are able to tolerate strong feelings, uncertainty and muddle and who can help children make sense of their feelings and find words for them. Educational psychotherapists always stay in role, are predictable in their responses and hold the memory of previous sessions. They value the child's creations and will take care of them during the gaps between sessions.

The children in the studies were initially far from experiencing the educational psychotherapist in this way and while psychotherapists hold onto the aim of fostering a healthy attachment relationship they take careful note of how the child does in fact perceive them. Do they, for instance, expect the psychotherapist to be critical, demanding, rivalrous, fragile, protective or preoccupied with personal concerns? In order to observe the transference clearly educational psychotherapists avoid giving personal information that might influence their views.

Educational psychotherapists also pay attention to the feelings that children elicit in them. Some children evoke protective feelings or despair. Others may irritate or enrage. Osman's therapist had to resist initial feelings of depression, helplessness and hopelessness when she was in the room with him. The feelings a child evokes can be an indication of feelings he may be struggling with himself. One teacher said that a boy made her feel hopeful and then let down. Later she discovered that the child's foster placements kept breaking down. He was vividly but unconsciously letting her know about his own experience.

It is particularly important for educational psychotherapists to be aware of and resist the pressure on them to respond in certain ways so that they can give a child a different experience of relating to an adult. They are open and alert to children's emotional state and communications at the same time as they continue to think objectively about them. From the outset they demonstrate the capacity to stay with painful or anxiety-provoking feelings rather than offering reassurance. We saw how, despite Osman's distress on being left alone with his therapist, she persevered, demonstrating her belief that difficult feelings could be manageable.

Staying with painful realities can be a challenge for a teacher who is accustomed to taking a positive stance. However it is ultimately more reassuring to a child to have his worries named and faced. He may otherwise feel that nobody can bear the reality of the situation. Comments such as 'Perhaps it might be hard to believe you will become a reader . . . ' are useful because they both acknowledge the hopeless feelings and express hopefulness at the same time.

When meeting children it is useful to establish why they think they are coming to the clinic or being assessed. What are their 'stories' about themselves and their educational struggle? Insecurely attached children tend to lack a coherent narrative of their own experience. It is common for children with longstanding histories of educational failure and emotional difficulties to wonder whether they are bad or even mad. Reflecting back these feelings and concerns 'contains' anxiety and sets the scene for a deeper level of communication. This establishes the ethos of the therapy and conveys the opportunity for a new and different kind of learning experience.

Clarification of the nature of the clinical sessions is important – for example, explaining what kind of information would be useful and how the assessment will be used and fed back to others. Adolescents, in particular, can be responsive to a discussion about different reasons for problems in school and the way in which they will have an opportunity to understand more about their particular responses to learning. Anxious children may like to be given a concrete idea of what happens in a session.

In the first session educational psychotherapists will let the child know that this is a confidential and private space – but that if they have concerns about the child's safety they will need to tell someone in the network. This may be equally relevant in school where individual work of a confidential nature is taking place. This issue is discussed in detail in Chapter 5.

The assessment should ideally take place in the same quiet room each time. Deprived children may be overwhelmed by too many materials or activities on offer – as may hyperactive children – and so it is often useful to have a limited selection of materials available. Apart from test materials this might include pens, pencils, Sellotape, drawing paper, storybooks and a game or two.

ASSESSING ACADEMIC STRENGTHS AND WEAKNESSES

On a practical level, before they can consider why the problem arose and what maintains it, educational psychotherapists will need to pinpoint the educational difficulty, establish a baseline learning level and confirm an emotional component to the problem. She wants to know about basic skills in numeracy, literacy and expressive and receptive language – including what the child can achieve with support. The latter is particularly important because incapacity to use a teacher is a crucial part of the assessment and the work. The teacher may also want to screen for undiagnosed specific learning difficulties – for instance weaknesses in visual or auditory perception or memory. These will not be described in detail in this book.

Assessing emotional developmental age is important. Tools such as the Draw a Person Test (Harris, 1963), which give an indication of a child's emotional developmental age, are useful in measuring progress if administered before and after the therapy. Children are asked to draw their 'best' drawing of a person and the drawing is then scored according to the number of bodily features they include compared to other children of the same age. Establishing whether the child has reached a stage of play consistent with formal learning is also necessary. The stages of play (Winnicott, 1971a, 1971b) were illustrated in the study about Osman and are outlined in Chapter 7.

Recreating the conditions that the child will encounter in school – some direct task work in a setting reminiscent of the classroom – allows educational psychother- apists to observe the child's response to formal teaching. Very close attention to re- sponses to the task helps them to gain insight. Osman's therapist noticed how he was unable to join up the fences despite the fact that it was similar to the way in which the 'Connect Four' frame fitted together. She concluded that he had a limited capacity for the transfer of skills and to holding onto skills learned.

A child's reaction to learning activities that are familiar, unfamiliar, challenging, easy, closed-ended or open-ended is interesting. Ego strengths will be noted – for instance the child's capacity to persevere, ask for help, bear making mistakes and allow time to complete work. A method devised by Ann-Marit Sletten Duve (1998) a psychologist and a pioneer of educational psychotherapy in Norway, is particularly useful for assessing a child's ego functioning.

OBSERVING DEFENSIVE BEHAVIOUR

Osman, when faced with activities and tasks, attempted to deal with the intense anxiety in a number of ways. He initially avoided connecting with his therapist or any activities requiring an emotional response. He was reluctant to ask for help and instead adopted a controlling, omnipotent stance as 'it was unbearable for him to be helped because that implied not knowing and it seemed that for Osman not knowing aroused feelings of helplessness . . . ' In addition he persevered with 'mindless' play in order to shut his therapist out and fill up the space himself.

Troubled children use a variety of ways to manage difficult feelings arising from educational challenges and relating to a teacher. Some use constant movement and activity to keep thinking at bay and others escape painful realities by going into a world of their own. Some regress, adopting a helpless stance. Others project uncomfortable feelings into another person – so that, for instance, it is the therapist who is seen as getting things all wrong. Splitting off unwanted aspects of self and locating them elsewhere is a commonly used defence but can impede learning.

Another child in educational psychotherapy, Mary, drew a picture of an abusive adult male. She depicted him alongside a drawing of herself and a drawing of an imaginary friend. The latter was given many features common to the human figure drawings of sexually abused children. So bad feelings were split off and located in the friend. By doing so, Mary was also able to keep a picture of herself as healthy and free of abuse This way of disowning painful feelings, however, leads to a rigid com- partmentalization of thoughts and ultimately to a difficulty in integrating information. Making connections in her mind was simply too dangerous.

Much of the behaviour of troubled children in the classroom is a defence against painful feelings. One child, who had become the classroom clown, was able to articulate this saying that when he made the class laugh 'they forget I can't spell.' Teachers need to be alert to the way that children 'share out' aspects of themselves in class, lodging characteristics in individual pupils. It is all too easy to let one child carry the 'comic misbehaviour' for the group.

The behaviour of insecure children in the classroom, of course, is frequently related to managing the relationship with the teacher. Teachers must be alert to this and how the child may use the task defensively to control them – for example to engage their attention or to avoid them. Awareness of a child's attachment history and the way this translates into the classroom can be very helpful (Geddes, 2006).

ATTACHMENT PATTERNS AND THE CHILD IN THE CLASSROOM

From birth, children's feelings of safety and wellbeing depend on keeping close to their carers in both a physical and psychological sense. John Bowlby (1969) was important in developing understanding of this and wrote seminal books on the subject of attachment and separation. In these he highlighted the effects on children of adverse experiences within their families.

Later researchers identified some of the ways that children attempt to manage their relationships with their carers in order to keep close to them. Ainsworth and Wittig (1969) devised the 'Strange Situation test' to observe a toddler's reaction to separation from the mother and his behaviour towards her on reunion. On the basis of this they categorized the children's habitual 'attachment patterns'. Main and Solomon (1982) later extended this classification.

When a child bonds well with a mother who is closely attuned to him and responsive to his needs he develops a secure attachment to her. The link between the quality of early emotional experience with the mother and learning development is well established. Murray et al. (1993) for instance, demonstrated how young children with depressed mothers who were self-engrossed and less able to focus on the children's experience did less well on cognitive tests than their counterparts who had healthy mothers. Securely attached children who have 'internalized' a reliable maternal figure tend to experience the teacher as helpful and feel confident enough to work independently.

As a rule, the children seen in educational psychotherapy are 'anxiously attached'. Anxiously attached children fall into three distinct categories based on the strategies they use to manage the relationship with a significant adult.

A child who has experienced a consistently rejecting carer may present as 'avoidant' – ignoring the teacher as far as possible and clinging to a belief that he can be self-sufficient. Such children are generally not very verbally communicative and tend to express hostility indirectly through the task. The teacher sees that this defence, used by the child to manage unbearable feelings and arising from the experience of a parent who was unavailable to him, now creates a difficulty for the child in acknowledging or allowing the teacher to be helpful.

Children who have an unpredictable parent are more likely to present as 'resistant' or 'ambivalent'. Their way of coping with carers who are not consistently available is both to cling to them and to angrily reject them. In class they behave in a way that keeps the teacher's attention on them at all times. They are overtly hostile towards the teacher and resistant to being taught. Schoolwork is often used manipulatively to engage the teacher. Such children tend to be more verbal and articulate than 'avoidant' children. They pay more attention to attachment-related information and find it hard to focus on work. For this reason the educational psychotherapy may require more time because the child needs to be helped to a stage where he or she can temporarily cut off from the adult and engage in the schoolwork. It is interesting that Kevin (Chapter 8) first became interested in letter sounds in relation to the names of rival children who came to the clinic.

A third and smaller category of anxiously attached children are called 'disorganized'. These children may have had carers who were frightened or frightening or suffering from mental health problems or drug abuse. They have not been able to find a consistent way of managing the relationship with carers. In class they are described by teachers as 'all over the place', 'highly volatile and unpredictable' or 'cut off, and unreachable'. Quite frequently these children have developed a defensively punitive or care-taking controlling stance with their parents. This behaviour may then be replicated in the classroom. Such children present an enormous challenge to adults working with them, who must provide a highly consistent and safe environment. The reader may wonder whether Tariq (Chapter 6) falls into this category.

NEUROLOGICAL FACTORS

Recently there has been considerable interest in the effect that the quality of attachment experience has on a child's developing brain. Substantial evidence from neurobiological research indicates that very early interpersonal experiences inform the selective development of neural pathways within the brain and nervous system (Balbernie, 2001). Healthy attachment relationships foster learning and repeated good experiences with an attuned and reflective carer leads to the formation of a well organized, well regulated 'baby mind' (Schore, 1994). The outcome is an individual who has a strong sense of self and agency.

When considering 'disorganized' children in particular, the psychotherapist is aware of the neurological implications of lack of containment and chronic early trauma. In brief, the use-dependent nature of brain development can mean that if a young child is exposed to chronic trauma the part of the brain that responds to survival threat becomes overdeveloped at the expense of the parts of the brain responsible for reflection and emotional regulation. Children who have witnessed or experienced traumatic events can hold these in implicit, 'procedural' rather than 'semantic' memory. The memories cannot be remembered in words but are held in a bodily memory. When children are in a context reminiscent of the traumatic one, they may respond with fear or panic and react with 'fight, flight, freeze' responses common to individuals faced with perceived life-threatening situations. Because of their vulnerability due to age and size, fight is not always an option – so flight or freeze responses are more common.

The child develops heightened sensitivity to situations perceived as threatening and may be overly responsive to small hidden triggers in the environment. When teachers notice extreme behaviours in pupils and those behaviours appear to come from nowhere, it may be that a procedural memory was triggered by an expression on the teacher's face, the sound of a distant siren and so on. Perry (1999) says that the traumatized child 'may be sitting in a classroom in a persistent state of arousal or anxiety, or dissociated. In either case the child is essentially unavailable to process efficiently the complex cognitive information being conveyed by the teacher.'

The realization that children's alarming and 'inexplicable' behaviour has a logical origin helps the teacher to manage her own responses. The teacher may also be able to help children to develop an awareness of the triggers to their behaviour, through close monitoring and observation. It is heartening to remember that children's brains continue to develop and that positive experiences at school can be beneficial.

LOOKING FOR CLUES: THE UNCONSCIOUS MEANING OF THE TASK OR ACTIVITY

The studies show how, because of their symbolic nature, reading, writing, maths and other subjects can become the arena for the expression of emotional difficulties for insecure children. Learning, as we have said, begins within the first relationship with the carer and unconscious phantasies arising from infantile experiences around feeding and relating can mean that the processes and content in learning and the relationship with the teacher can become imbued with special meaning. Unconscious ideas have a profound impact on learning in ways not easily observable. Moreover, children who have had a difficult start are especially vulnerable to later adverse experiences.

Children find an infinite variety of ways to convey information that may be held in implicit memory and not necessarily available for expression in words. They do this through their approach to tasks and activities, the content of their creations and also through their response to the adult teaching them. The clues they give enable the observant teacher to gain important insights. There follow some examples of this from other children in educational psychotherapy.

Ten-year-old William, who had a poor relationship with his mother and had witnessed chronic domestic violence, was totally passive in the learning environment. He had unconsciously equated the aggression necessary for tackling tasks with hurtful violence. He may also have been carrying his mother's projections about potent masculinity being dangerous. This anxiety impacted on his capacity to read. He dared not break words into their component sounds because he despaired of ever putting them together again.

Information felt to be illicit can inhibit learning too. Bowlby (1988) wrote about how children whose reality has been denied may not be able to trust their own senses and perceptions.

Sam had progressed very well academically and was ready to read but seemed to stop in his tracks, refusing to take the next step. In the first assessment session he drew his entire family including all his siblings. One brother, however, was depicted with wings rather than arms. Exploration with his family revealed a 'secret' supposedly unknown by the child – that this brother was suffering from a terminal illness. Reading is about independent access to knowledge and stumbling across information felt to be dangerous and taboo set up an internal conflict for this boy.

Unresolved loss can be a factor in learning difficulty. Phyllis Blanchard (1946) found that more than half the children she assessed with reading inhibitions had experienced significant loss. Loss often impacts on numeracy skills too. Shamira, struggling with issues around the death of significant family members, found subtraction impossible to master.

Claire, who had suffered loss and illness in her family and had to support her fragile mother, was inhibited about having a go at tasks in school. She seemed to believe that she would deplete or destroy the educational psychotherapist/teacher with her demands as a learner. In her sessions she watched her therapist's face anxiously to see if she was upset by her mistakes, worried about breaking the pen and messing up her exercise book. She drew her family with the use of a ruler in an attempt at rigid control – as if free expression might be disastrous. She depicted herself with hands behind her back – a typical feature of children worried about hostile impulses. Claire needed to experience a teacher who demonstrated robustness and a capacity to bear her mistakes, hostility and messy feelings.

Some immature children have a poor grasp of symbolism affecting their capacity to manage aspects of learning. We saw how Osman reacted with acute anxiety when faced with certain texts. When children have no secure sense of themselves as separate from their carers, they have no basis for sublimation and so an object, such as a wolf in a story, is experienced as the real thing. One child was afraid to read the word 'lion' in case it bit her.

The mistakes children make in their work can be informative. Misreadings, for example, may have significance beyond a mechanical reading difficulty. One child, for instance, always read 'monster' instead of 'mother'. Another was unable to spell his surname correctly despite good spelling capacity and lots of practice.

Performance in straightforward tests cannot always be taken at face value as an indicator of ability. For example one child's paralysis when faced with a spelling test was a consequence of his overwhelming desire to please the tester. His therapist also noted that he had extreme difficulty in joining up his writing and she later linked this to his difficulty in joining up with his new foster family. A third child clearly confused making a mistake in the test with making a mess. One girl was so consumed with envy of the therapist who had all the knowledge and power that she refused to cooperate at all.

EXPRESSION WORK, CURRICULUM SUBJECTS AND PROJECTIVE TESTS

Curriculum subjects and creative activities, such as story making, drawing and play allow children to express and explore ideas and conflicts. This helps adults to gain insight into their inner world and the way this marries with outside reality. Working through the metaphor in this way comes naturally to teachers and respects a child's defences. Children reveal a great deal about their personal experiences and relationships in their written material and the teacher must always pay attention to the content and consider both what this says about the child and whether this is an important communication. One child wrote a vivid description in response to the request for an essay on bullying. He was given an 'A' but later attempted suicide.

Children sometimes find their own metaphors for their concerns. Preoccupation with external events can be telling. One child, for instance, who was not supposed to know that his father was in prison, was obsessed with drawing and writing about *Who Framed Roger Rabbit?* A teenage girl who was full of repressed fury towards her stepfather, was fascinated by the potentially disastrous effects of a nuclear explosion. In a similar way the choice of books and other materials as well as particular activities causing anxiety or enthusiasm, can be significant.

Educational psychotherapists commonly use a range of projective materials and tests to gain information about the child's view of the world – some of which can be scored and others used impressionistically. Teachers can adapt and create their own material based on these ideas – particularly when standardized scores are not required. Some tests, such as the sentence completion test and 'Draw A Person', are easily administered to a class group and can highlight areas requiring further investigation.

The Children's Apperception Test (Bellack, 1949) asks for responses to shadowy visual scenarios and can show how overtly well-behaved children may be highly disturbed, deprived or harbour violent phantasies. In a similar way the Madeleine Thomas (1937) stories describe everyday scenarios that take place at home or school and ask the child to say what they think has happened or will happen. Paul Rosenzweig (1948) devised an activity using unelaborated drawings of people interacting. Empty speech bubbles invited the child to guess how one person may respond to the other and write the words in the empty space.

Adolescents often tend to respond better to more 'structured' materials. For instance, they might give information about themselves through questions about what their friends would say about them – or sentence completion exercises. When facilitating the expression of feelings and thoughts in words the educational psychotherapist keeps communication open-ended, avoiding direct questions that require 'yes' or 'no' answers. Reflecting back a child's comments – or 'wondering how it feels' – encourages further communication.

The educational psychotherapist who uses a familiar set of assessment materials and tools with a range of children can make useful comparisons and pick out unusual responses. Assessors, however, will have their own preferred repertoires of expressive materials and activities. Being an experienced teacher is advantageous in that such a teacher will have a good idea of typical responses from children at certain ages and can be alert to differences.

DRAWINGS

Drawings play a very important part in the work as a diagnostic tool, a measure of progress, and above all, a nonverbal means through which children can express, explore and convey thoughts and feelings. The content of children's drawings carries both conscious and unconscious material and can be very revealing. There is always a subjective aspect in interpreting these, however, and it is very important that drawings are never used as the sole evidence of any diagnosis and are only part of a multifaceted assessment.

On an impressionistic level, aspects of drawings such as the colour, boldness, movement and emotional impact of drawings and paintings can convey a sense of a child's feeling state. Depressed children, for example, may use a great deal of black and over scribbling. Children with low self-esteem often depict themselves very tiny and use faint colours.

Human figure drawings, as we have seen in the studies, can convey information about children's views of themselves in relation to others and to their environment. Koppitz maintained that any human figure drawing by a child is a reflection of the child's inner representation of self. An example of this is a large pubertal boy who depicted himself as a pretty ballerina in pink. This led to a discussion that revealed his gender conflict. Another child drew himself 'stuck' to his identical twin. Subsequent work revealed his difficulties in having a separate identity.

In addition to using these human figure drawings impressionistically, standardized scales can provide information on cognitive and emotional developmental age that can supplement information measured verbally. The Draw a Person test has already been mentioned. Other scales using emotional indicators yield information on the nature or severity of children's anxieties (Koppitz, 1968). It is useful when considering human figure drawings to also ask children for drawings that preclude affect such as geometrical shapes, to distinguish between problems related to, say, coordination, perception and emotional factors.

Some research indicates that the emotional developmental age of human figure drawings may pinpoint the age at which a child suffered a trauma or environmental lapse (Moore, 1990). This is because the child may have split off feelings found to be unbearable at the time. In addition it is helpful to know that certain indicators in these drawings are common to groups of children with particular difficulties such as sexual abuse, learning difficulties and ADHD. For example, children with ADHD tend to put extra objects into their drawings and they tend to draw people with heads embedded into the body – as if there is no distance between thought and action (Moore, 1995). Children who have been prescribed the medication Ritalin tend to produce more integrated drawings than those not taking the medication. Knowledge about drawings, therefore, in conjunction with information from other sources, can alert the psychotherapist to possibilities about the nature of a child's problems. Readers wishing to know more about children's drawings may find a book by Cathy Malchiodi (1998) useful and accessible.

Kinetic family drawings, as already illustrated, are commonly used in the assessment. Children are asked to draw their families 'doing something'. The results can be highly informative in terms of who is included or excluded, the interaction of family members, the position of the child in relation to others and so on. Research indicates that some features of these drawings can indicate a child's attachment pattern. Like human figure drawings, the House Tree and Person test (Buck, 1996) tends to indicate many projective aspects of the self and also gives interesting insights.

Drawings also provide an excellent opportunity for educational psychotherapist and child to engage in mutual creative play. The Squiggle game (Winnicott, 1971a, 1971b) and shared drawings are examples of this. In the former, the psychotherapist responds to a quick scribble made by the child, turning it into something. Then the child does the same. This immediately puts the adult and the child on an equal footing. In addition, as there are no 'wrong' responses, it indicates to the child that his unique view of things is valid.

The changes in children's drawings over the course of the work can be a measure of progress. The drawings often become more integrated and carry better narrative content as the therapy continues.

STORIES AND PLAY

Children's own dictated or written stories are a rich source of information about the nature of their attachments and their views of themselves and the world. Secure children's stories tend to be coherent and have a beginning, middle and resolution. The characters are benign and have a sense of agency. In contrast, insecure children produce less coherent stories. In the case of 'disorganized' children these might be characterized by extreme violence, catastrophe and magical or no solutions. Alternatively the children may be extremely inhibited about story making.

If children are inhibited about making stories, semi-structured means of eliciting these can be helpful. These can include such materials as the Madeleine Thomas Stories already mentioned. Some educational psychotherapists find that the standardized Story Stems devised by the Anna Freud Institute can be a particularly useful diagnostic tool concerning children's attachment representations. The adult acts out the beginning of a story using small animals and dolls and the child completes the story. Picture cards can be useful stimuli too and sometimes can be offered as a sequence if more structure is called for. Using the same set of pictures with many children means that comparisons can be made. Other interactive means of eliciting story making include the use of speech bubbles and paper 'conversations' that take place between therapist and child. Some children prefer to do this in role as someone else. For instance they might choose to be animals.

Children's own choice of books can be revealing. Kevin (Chapter 8) chose *The Very Hungry Caterpillar*, who, no matter how much he eats, still feels hungry. This reflected his greed and emptiness borne of deprivation. Tariq, (Chapter 6) persecuted by his own projected monstrous feelings, expressed his hopefulness about help when he chose *Where The Wild Things Are* about a boy who becomes King of the Wild Monsters and tames them.

Some fearful children prefer to create their own stories rather than being at the mercy of text that is not their own and may contain something they do not wish to hear. It sometimes takes time before children who happily make a story can share the task with their therapist – particularly if they have not yet attained the stage of mutual play. As with drawings, the change in children's stories over the course of time can be a measure of their emotional development.

Play and learning are closely connected. Observing a child's capacity for play is highly important in the assessment and the work. We saw how Osman had a poor capacity for symbolic play and it took a great deal of time before he could engage in a playful interaction in his therapy. Playfulness and play are an integral part of the closely attuned reciprocal mother/infant relationship vital to healthy attachment (Schore, 1994). If, as a consequence of early adverse experience, playfulness is inhibited, the child's capacity to learn will be compromised.

Aspects of children's play can inform us about hopes and fears. Osman identifies with the toy dog separating it from other animals. His therapist understands this in terms of his separating off bits of himself in order to detach himself from chaotic feelings that might overwhelm him. Maria's (Chapter 4) eagerness for games such as *Where's Wally* and hide and seek, seems linked to a desire to be found after being lost – and, perhaps, to have her hidden self known. Her play with miniature mixed-race dolls was an attempt to clarify issues around identity and loyalty. Many children in educational psychotherapy use sand play very fruitfully. Marion Milner has said that children seem especially aware of the symbolic nature of sand play within a frame. A fuller discussion of the different stages of play (Winnicott, 1971a, 1971b) is given in Chapter 7.

The assessment, as we have seen, is a complex and challenging process. A number of techniques have been described that allow the educational psychotherapist to understand more about the reasons for the child's failure to learn. The therapist will select those activities and tests that seem appealing and relevant to the child and give a comprehensive view of his functioning in an educational context. If the outcome leads to ongoing educational psychotherapy then further elucidation of the nature of his difficulties remains integral to the work.

THE ASSESSMENT PROCEDURE

As we have seen, children referred for educational psychotherapy fail to make optimal use of educational opportunities in school despite extra support offered there. At the time of referral there can be a high level of despair and bewilderment both in the children and the adults trying to help them.

In school the children may be:

- unhappy, preoccupied, depressed or withdrawn;
- unable to express thoughts and feelings;
- restless, overactive and unable to concentrate;
- expressing emotions through violent or disruptive behaviour;
- struggling with aspects of the curriculum or basic skills;
- having difficulty relating to teachers or peers.

Many of the children have experienced disrupted relationships, loss or trauma arising from abuse, neglect or violence and lack of continuity of care. Recent research by the NSPCC confirms the link between adverse home experiences of this kind and learning difficulty. Some otherwise secure children may have specific difficulties relating to an aspect of learning or respond to a temporary environmental lapse through arrested learning.

Referrals for educational psychotherapy come from health or education professionals, social services or parents. These typically arise at times of transition because vulnerable children are more likely to find loss, change and new beginnings challenging. The referrals provide information and enable a hypothesis to be formed about the child's difficulties, alerting the therapist to questions that should be asked.

As discussed in Chapter 5, factors sometimes emerge during an assessment that indicate ongoing work is not advisable or appropriate. Deprived children may be so tantalized by the intimacy offered that they cannot cope. One such child became unmanageable, 'trashing' the psychotherapy room whenever he realized the end of the session was close. He was ultimately offered intensive psychotherapy. Another child revealed current maltreatment at home. This was not severe enough to warrant a child protection referral but by continuing the work the therapist could be seen as condoning the situation.

It is common for referred children to have parents with significant mental health problems and some children may feel disloyal or distressed by an invitation to engage with a reflective, healthy adult. Sometimes, too, children are so preoccupied with the relationship with the therapist that they are unlikely to use teaching materials at all. Such a child may do better in child psychotherapy. Other children are found to have undiagnosed specific learning difficulties and may benefit from an alternative specialist teaching. There is, of course, a significant overlap in children with difficulties such as ADHD and dyslexia and those with emotional problems and many educational psychotherapists work with such children. In most cases a child who is assessed for educational psychotherapy is offered ongoing work.

The assessment usually requires three or four individual sessions with a child preceded by a meeting with the family. This meeting may include the referred child, parents and siblings and the therapist and co-worker. The co-worker may or may not offer the parents appointments during the assessment period.

It is important that another professional in the service maintains contact with the family to support the work with the child. This ensures against sabotage of the work by parents who may themselves be needy or envious and also provides a vehicle for the sharing of important information about the child's outside world so that the boundaries around the child's sessions are protected.

Similarly, in a school setting where regular individual special needs help is being offered, it may be helpful if another member of staff deals with disciplinary matters involving the child, and possibly also links with the family. This is particularly important for older children who need to feel that they can trust the privacy of the work.

The initial family meeting provides the opportunity to:

- Take a family and developmental history. This would include a history of significant losses, separation, illness, emigration and family mental health issues. It helps establish the context within which the educational difficulty began.
- Observe family interactions in terms of a possible link with the child's difficulty. An example of this was a father who criticized his son for failing to speak out in the meeting but was scornful whenever he did so.
- Assess motivation for change in the family. Sometimes the referrer and other outside agencies may be anxious about a child but if the child's difficulty is serving a purpose in the family, such as diverting attention from marital difficulties, the family may resist change.
- Explain the nature of the work to the child and the parents and set up a working alliance with them.
- Make practical plans for the educational assessment sessions.
- Obtain permission to contact school and other agencies.

After the assessment is complete there is another meeting with the family to share information and to make plans for further intervention. Here the educational psychotherapist will give an initial formulation of the difficulty and say how the child made use of the sessions. She will have spoken to the child already about what he or she intends to say. Great care is needed when feeding back some aspects of the child's communications. For instance, rather than giving details about the distressing parental marital rows heard about in the sessions, the therapist may say that the child is someone who is highly sensitive to disharmony at home.

As mentioned before, the feedback of an assessment, particularly of a child who has had chronic and perplexing difficulties, can reframe the problem in a helpful way. One child's parents were able to be far more accepting of their son's poor progress in literacy when his 'resistance to trying' was interpreted instead as a deep fear of getting anything wrong.

The most useful time to visit the school is at the end of the assessment process. Educational psychotherapists are then in a position to share their own observations of the child with the teacher. They need to be aware of confidentiality issues when doing so and will have ascertained that the child and his family are in agreement with the visit and the communications they make.

Having a personal sense of the child informs educational psychotherapists in gathering information from school staff to supplement their own. In particular they will want to know about a child's behaviour in a group situation and the child's relationship to peers and adults. They may ask the teacher to fill in the teachers' version of the Goodman Strengths and Difficulties Questionnaire or other such forms. This not only provides information but also serves as a means of measuring change if it can be readministered at the end of therapy. Building in a means of 'audit' is useful in all special needs intervention. Asking teachers to identify changes that they would like to see in the child in class can be useful.

It is important to hold in mind that teachers may have mixed feelings about the therapist. Teachers struggling with a large group of pupils may feel understandably envious of the opportunity to work individually with a child. They may be unclear about the nature of the therapeutic work and feel excluded from information about the family. The therapist can usefully share information about the activities and adapted teaching that makes up a typical session and acknowledge the challenge for the teacher in managing a child in the context of a whole class. Making a good alliance is enormously helpful to both teacher and therapist. In addition, when teachers become interested in the therapist's ideas, this can benefit all the children in the class.

One teacher who had become embattled with a child who 'rubbished' her efforts to teach him or accept her authority was helped to understand that his belief that he could manage on his own was necessary to his sense of safety and survival. Seeing his behaviour as reflecting his past experience rather than a personal failure in their interaction enabled her to step back out of the conflict and respond less punitively. Once she stopped feeling overwhelmed by his behaviour and conveyed instead a wish to make sense of it, the boy felt 'contained' and he became less oppositional. Supporting the adults involved with the child's development is an important part of the educational psychotherapist's work and throughout the therapy contact with the school will be maintained.

It is clear that an assessment of this kind in clinic or school can clarify the nature of the difficulty and, whether or not educational psychotherapy is seen as suitable, can helpfully inform the teacher about classroom organization and approaches. Teachers sometimes report that children find the experience of being the focus of an assessment can in itself be beneficial.

4 Case Study of Maria, Whose Learning is Inhibited by Rejection, Separation and Loss

In this study, Dorothy Wickson tells the story of her work with a withdrawn eight-year-old girl who had suffered loss and separation. Maria is a child with an 'internal working model' of herself as unlovable and unwanted. Her educational psychotherapist notes how she 'drifts off' into her own world and understands this in terms of her preoccupation with anxious thoughts, memories and feelings. These intrude in unhelpful ways and before she can focus on learning the anxieties need to be addressed through play, stories and the relationship with the therapist. Maria uses the opportunities offered to explore her hostile feelings towards her attachment figures, her confusion about her racial identity and her fear of abandonment. She does this almost entirely at one remove with very little direct discussion. The experience of an adult who consistently holds her in mind and bears the expression of negative feelings enables her to re-engage with learning and facilitates her emotional development.

INTRODUCTION

Maria is eight years old and has two older sisters. Her Irish mother and Indian father had divorced by the time she was two years old. The family was referred to the clinic because the middle daughter, Rose (nine years old), had eating difficulties. When they attended the clinic, however, it became apparent that there were further concerns. The mother, Ms O, was depressed. Cara, the eldest daughter, was approaching adolescence and her behaviour was deteriorating and Maria the youngest was described as 'not doing very well' in school. There were many family arguments and fights and mother was battling through the courts with her husband who was attempting to gain contact with his daughters.

My colleague, a psychiatric social worker (PSW), first saw the family. Ms O was very worried about her daughters and thought that the family's problems were the result of the traumatic breakdown of the marriage. The PSW met Maria, the youngest daughter, on two occasions and recognized that she could benefit from educational psychotherapy because she was underachieving in school and seemed ready to talk to her in the sessions. I was asked to see Maria and began work with her in May of that year. She has now been in educational psychotherapy for 13 months and has attended regularly.

FAMILY BACKGROUND

I learned, from the PSW who had met Ms O with her children, that Ms O had a very unhappy childhood herself. Her father had behaved violently towards her mother and had rejected their youngest child. This had affected her mother deeply and driven her to addiction and neglect of her children. In contrast Ms O had endeavoured to be a good mother to her children. She had married a man older than herself who seemed stable and kind but who became possessive and jealous once they were married.

Ms O found that she was pregnant again less than a year after the birth of her second child but her husband threatened to leave her if she terminated the pregnancy. Following Maria's birth, her mother suffered from postnatal depression and had recurring bouts of depression thereafter. Acrimonious court battles resulted in an order prohibiting Mr P from any contact with the family. Ms O then changed their name to her own family name.

Several years before I met Maria, their father, who was by then divorced from his wife, had taken his eldest daughter, Cara, to his homeland (India) and left her in the care of his family while he returned to England. Over a year later Mr P still refused to allow Cara home. After many requests for her return and upsetting phone calls from her daughter Ms O left her two younger daughters in the care of a friend and went to India to bring Cara back. Three years later, Mr. P again attempted to snatch Cara away and take her back to India. After that there was then no contact with Mr. P for about two years although, recently, Cara had made contact with her father.

SCHOOL SITUATION

Maria was two years and six months old when she first attended a children's centre. She then went to the nursery class in the local school and was in year 2 when I met her. At this time Ms O was in discussion with the school regarding Maria's lack of progress and had let the head know about her concerns and worries. She became increasingly dissatisfied with the amount of help the school was prepared to give and planned to move Maria and her older sister Rose to a new school at the end of the academic year.

I visited the first school, not knowing at the time that Maria was going to move. The class teacher was worried about her and said she was 'not sure whether Maria's learning difficulty was low intelligence or something else'. She talked about Maria's behaviour in class and said she seemed to be unable to operate in a large group. She said, 'She can't follow instructions and is quite disruptive in her own way.' She clarified this as 'chatting and being a bit of a nuisance.' She said that there had always been concerns about Maria.

Two months later, when Maria began her new school, I visited it. This school was a small faith school. This meant a slightly longer journey for the family but mother was pleased that the children were able to go there. When I met the head teacher for the first time she threw her arms up in despair, saying, 'What are we going to do with her?' She described Maria as a 'brick wall', a 'typical daydreamer.' She baffled and confused her and the teachers also felt they could not understand her. At this time Maria was seriously behind her peers in her learning, particularly in reading, writing, spelling and maths.

The story of the work with Maria follows a chronological order.

THE ASSESSMENT PERIOD

I first met Maria in May when she had been coming to the clinic with her mother and sisters for three months. At our first meeting, which included her mother, Maria smiled and lowered her head. I was, however, encouraged by the inquisitive way she looked at me through the corner of her eye. Her Mother did most of the talking for Maria who only spoke when asked to, looking again to mother for confirmation. Ms O listed all the things that she felt Maria was having difficulty with – spelling, reading, lack of concentration and an inability to hold information in her head. She could not count to 100, or in 2s, 5s or 10s! Ms O also mentioned dyspraxia and some time later in the year she went to see a paediatrician about this. The subsequent report indicated no concerns.

I invited Maria to have a look around the educational psychotherapy room. She found it difficult to go up to things, glanced around, stood close to mother and at one point was touching her hair. She appeared to need to take care of her mother who told me that she thought there might be emotional reasons for Maria's difficulties related to early childhood experiences.

In the first assessment session I talked to Maria about a drawing that she had made recently with the family worker. She had drawn a sun, a sunflower, and a figure. The picture was beautifully edged with a decorative border and she had written her name neatly and clearly across the top using different colours. I asked her to tell me about it. She told me that the little girl was angry with the sunflower. The picture was full of happy smiling faces, but her comment that the girl was angry, seemed to reveal hidden feelings. I noticed that Maria looked happy and smiling, like the picture, and wondered if beneath the happy exterior was an angry and unhappy little girl.

Bearing in mind that Maria had been rejected at birth and not wanted by a mother who then had postnatal depression it seemed possible, as the picture seemed to indicate, that Maria idealized her mother, showing her in the form of a happy smiling sunflower. I think she may have split off her hurt and angry feelings for a mother who was not there for her, and who could not protect her from an aggressive father. It seemed that Maria had been able to be in touch with these feelings, which lay below the surface, and tried to express them through her picture and comment. I wondered whether her reluctance to read might be an expression of her hostility to her mother who was so keen for 'her girls to do well'.

Maria's early experiences included the abduction of her sister, being left suddenly for a period of time by her mother – and a father who was indifferent to her. It seems likely that in denying angry and upset feelings arising from these experiences she might be in danger of creating a false self. This, in turn, might inhibit exploration and learning.

In the assessment period, I found that maths was Maria's biggest difficulty. She muddled the numbers and was confused by the numerals on the clock face. I wondered if this was because she was a member of a family whose number of members had not been constant. With people disappearing or not being there and with numbers in her household never being the same, not adding up – perhaps it was hard for her to know that numbers are constant and do not alter. However, she very quickly got to know at what time sessions began and ended.

Maria was thoughtful and organized in her approach to tasks. In individual sessions, she could ask for help but would also reject it and say, 'don't help me' or 'let me do it on my own'. Although she was struggling with maths, she was doing a little better in language. However, her reading was below her chronological age, her spellings were poor and she was generally underachieving in language. She struggled with and seemed unable to use reading strategies and clues that would help her. She had a good short-term memory in games such as Pelmanism, remembering where cards were replaced and taking them for herself next time! She had some difficulty with auditory discrimination, primarily initial consonant sounds. She seemed to enjoy drawing and her drawings were mostly age appropriate.

During this time, Maria also expressed negative thoughts about school. She stated that the teacher was unfair for accusing her of 'bullying and doing things she didn't do'. The teacher also made Maria sit near the back of the class, which she did not like.

I considered that Maria's first drawing and the comments she made were an early indication that she was able to work in the metaphor. I was hopeful that she would find a way in educational psychotherapy to begin to express and understand some of her feelings. I thought her eagerness to discuss her picture in the first session showed a wish to communicate with me and make a relationship. I was hopeful that, through this new trust, she would be able to develop more confidence in herself and her teachers and to feel freer to explore the possibilities of learning in school.

THE FIRST TERM – 'GETTING TO KNOW EACH OTHER'

After the assessment period, I began educational psychotherapy sessions with Maria in June. This meant that there would only be a few weeks before the long summer break.

To get to the room we had to walk through a long playroom. Maria would walk behind me, slightly dragging her feet and looking only ahead to where she was going.

In the beginning she would enter the room and sit down and look straight ahead of her. She would appear a little tense, not looking around the room. She spoke quietly and often I could not hear her or quite understand what she was saying. She accepted the educational task willingly and unquestioningly. She liked being told what to do, so she didn't have to think for herself.

Thinking was painful for Maria. She became muddled and confused but, most importantly, she put up a 'brick wall' as described by the head teacher – retreating behind it. She would stare ahead of her, looking blank, stop in mid-sentence, or she would say 'I don't know' or 'I can't remember'. It seemed sometimes as if she was having a conversation in her own head and not communicating her thoughts to others. At other times it was as if she expected me to know what was in her head. For example, when doing squiggle pictures she misunderstood my instructions to draw the line for me to turn into something – instead she thought I would draw a picture of what she had in *her* mind. She also played guessing games and asked one day 'guess which book I'm going to choose?'

It was too hard for Maria to take the initiative and to think and explore and she would often take the educational task that I had set into her own choosing time. I wondered if her difficulty in making decisions was related to her attachment to her mother. It was hard for Maria to separate and say goodbye to her mother at the beginning of sessions when they tended to kiss and wrap their arms around each other. Her mother always had something important she wanted to tell me. It felt intrusive of Maria's time and of Maria and perhaps indicated some resentment of her daughter. I thought that the enmeshed relationship with her mother might make it difficult for Maria to distinguish her thinking from her mother's. She might assume that the latter must know what she and everyone else was thinking. It was difficult for Maria to be able to step back out of that relationship and look at something objectively in a reflective way.

During an assessment session Maria had drawn a picture of her family. She depicted her grandmother as a blank circle without attempting to add any facial features. Her grandmother had died about a year before. This blank circle seemed to signify a number of things. The empty space left by a loss, loss of grandmother, and loss of an absent mother who, because of postnatal depression, was not there for Maria in her early years. It may also include the gaps when her mother disappeared to India to bring back her eldest daughter.

The 'brick wall' analogy again comes to mind when thinking about Maria and how when she entered the room, she sat down and looked blankly ahead, not moving or attempting to explore anything in the room. She appeared 'stuck' and 'frozen' to the chair. I thought about Winnicott's concept of a shared space to play and about 'reverie'. If at a critical early stage, Maria did not have access to a mother who could play with her or who was responsive to her gestures, then the desire to know, to search, to find out may have been affected. Maria seemed to have switched off and become unable to take anything in. This 'switching off' to ward off the hurt of an unavailable mother and the consequent mistrust of other adults such as teachers, had, I felt, limited and affected her ability to learn. She lacked the secure base from which to explore.

It became apparent as we moved closer to the first break that Maria needed to know clearly why I would not be there, that I would be coming back and that I was not abandoning her. I was hard pressed to contain her anxiety at the approaching break. During these weeks of initially getting to know each other Maria had come to idealize me. This was reminiscent of the way in which she dealt with negative feelings about her mother. She gave me a certificate with 'good Dorothy' written on it, which indicated that she still needed to be 'nice ' to me. But, during the next term our energies were generally to be spent getting to know each other better. She needed to know if I was trustworthy, if I would be there for her, if she could show me other kinds of feelings such as the 'bad bits' and if I would still accept her and like her at all costs.

I began to get a sense of where the focus of the work needed to be. I felt that there were three main difficulties to be tackled and understood. These included Maria's blanking and blocking out, her feelings of loss and abandonment and, thirdly, her inability to play and explore in a shared space. In the service of these aims the *Where's Wally?* books and hide-and-seek games had already been part of our sessions and proved to be important ways of communicating for us over the next term's work.

TERM 2 – 'MAKING AN ATTACHMENT'

Maria's experience of loss and separation in her early life made it very difficult for her to build a trusting relationship with me where she felt I would be available and accessible. As the educational psychotherapist I wanted to try to understand these difficult feelings of uncertainty and to give her a different experience of a reliable adult. After attending sessions for only a few weeks, the long summer break loomed. Maria would ask repeatedly 'Where are you going – are you coming back?' I found it hard to tolerate these painful feelings. It was not helpful to try to reassure her, but I will try to illustrate how, over the following term's work, I think Maria began to feel understood and how she began to make an attachment to me.

The anxiety about unreliable adults affected Maria's trust in teachers. If she could make a secure and trusting relationship with me then maybe this could transfer to the school situation where she might avail herself of what school and teachers had to give. She might then feel safer to be curious and to take risks in learning.

Maria returned after the long summer break. She had begun her new school and was coping with the changes. There were also changes at the clinic. Mother's family worker was leaving and was to be replaced by a new worker, a trainee child psychotherapist with supervision. 'Goodbyes' to her mother at the start of sessions still involved big wrap-around hugs and kisses and as her mother walked away Maria would seem to stick to her side and walk alongside her, touching her. I needed to remind her that she was coming with me and that I would return her to her mother later. However at the beginning of the penultimate session before Christmas, Maria touched her mother with her fingertips, as if she was slowly letting go and I noticed that hugs and kisses were decreasing.

I used a number of different educational tasks with Maria during this term. We began playing a Pelmanism game. She liked playing games and liked to win. She often accused me of cheating as though she was not sure that she could trust me. It seemed as though trust was an important question during this term and showed itself in a number of other interactions. At the end of one session she said, 'You really want to get rid of me, don't you?' I accepted this comment and acknowledged that it was hard to end and say goodbye and maybe it felt as though I wanted to get rid of her but that I would be there the following week.

Later in the term I started preparing Maria for the Christmas break. She immediately began splashing the yellow paint into the brown and then pretended to flick paint at me. I was again able to say how cross she was with me when I talked about the holiday. She began to laugh. I wondered what she was laughing about. She answered, 'Your face.' She had become very alert and watchful of my expression. This was partly a characteristic she had developed as a consequence of her experiences but also showed her anxiety about expressing hostility towards me on this occasion.

I used this material to talk about faces and expressions and what they can tell us. This implicitly indicated that I could accept and bear her angry feelings. The educational task for the next week arose from this exchange and involved a game of Fizzog (which involved matching faces). She kept the score. She tried different ways of doing this until she found a more accurate way. When we reached a score of 18 and 21, she asked, 'Who has the highest?' Later in the year, when playing and scoring another game Maria knew exactly who had the highest score and by how many! During this game she again asked 'Are you cheating?'

The box that held all Maria's work done during sessions became a testing ground for our relationship. We had previously had discussions about what the box was for and what it meant. One day, when questioning me about the box, she asked 'Are you the boss? Who says you can take things home or not?' I talked about the box being for Maria's things to be kept in safely at the clinic. Later on in the session she painted a picture and said, 'Oh, I'm doing this for my mum and I can't give it to her . . . oh!' I again talked about her box being a special safe place to leave things so that they would always be there. It seemed that Maria was beginning to feel safer about challenging my authority.

She began to find out that I could be trusted to keep her things safely at the clinic even if she was not happy about being unable to take home her picture. The box as a container had been challenged and now the room as a container was challenged!

Where's Wally? books and hide-and-seek games were part of almost every session. A few minutes each week of going through and finding Wally and a game of hide and seek to find Maria seemed to be a necessary part of the developing relationship and building up of trust. This may have been an important exploration of people who come and go and also, perhaps, about a desire for her true self to be found. When returning to the room one day she asked, 'Can we play hide and seek out of this room?' During choosing time she said 'Let's play hide and seek . . . but we have to stay in here don't we?' I was, again, given the opportunity to confirm to Maria that this was our special place and, although the room was small and not very interesting for playing hide and seek, it was the room where we spent our time together when she came to the clinic. I understood that the development of safe boundaries was very important for Maria because boundaries had been quite traumatically broken by her father.

As the Christmas break was almost upon us, Maria asked, 'Am I coming back . . . will it be in seven more days . . . will I be coming here when I am in year 5?' Then she added, 'I'm never going' and wrote my name on the blackboard. She had been trying to write this correctly over several weeks. On this occasion she did it correctly. I said 'Now you can remember how to spell my name, now you can remember me over the holidays!' She had something to take away with her and I felt that an attachment had been made.

TERM 3 – HIDE AND SEEK

I often thought about Maria as the 'forgotten child' who felt unseen and unheard. She was an unwanted pregnancy, being born only a year after her sister. Ms O had suffered postnatal depression and Maria was a cause of marital discord between Ms O and Mr P. During her mother's depression, father took over the caring role. When her mother was able to regain her role as caring for Maria, Ms O and Mr P separated. Subsequently, her father disappeared from Maria's life. Later on, as stated earlier, her mother disappeared to India to bring back Cara.

Maria had experienced a number of separations and losses in her young life. I wondered how this had made her feel. One indication was the first drawing that I described earlier and Maria's explanation 'that (girl) is angry with that flower.' Maria had angry feelings towards a mother who was not always there to take care of her and protect her, yet when they said goodbye to each other their behaviour appeared somewhat inappropriate, being too clingy and cuddly. It seemed that when saying goodbye to her mother, Maria could not quite believe that she would come back for her. She may also have worried about whether a farewell would be experienced as a rejection by her mother. Educational psychotherapy and games of hide and seek provided opportunities for feelings of loss and separation to be thought about. Similarly beginnings and endings of sessions became an important time.

Maria needed to be found. She needed to know that someone would look for her. She needed to look herself and to do the finding. She needed to know that she could still be thought about even if she couldn't be seen or heard. During one session she drew a picture of herself shouting her name into a microphone. (Her own words were, 'one of those things that make it sound loud'.) Comments from her teacher who said that she 'can be a bit of a nuisance' and Maria's own remarks about having to sit at the back of class (it's harder to be noticed at the back) indicate that she felt neither seen nor heard.

At the start of a session Maria would hide in the reception area while waiting for me to collect her. Then she would run on ahead and hide in the room. When the session ended and she was back in reception, she would hide from her mother. We played hide-and-seek games in sessions and I devised a number of other games around this theme as part of the educational task. Maria responded with absolute delight to these games and asked for them week after week. One of the games involved using miniature dolls. I had observed that when Maria first came to educational psychotherapy she seemed stuck and frozen to her chair and was not able to explore the room and find out what other materials and resources there were for her to use. I had also noticed that she did not play imaginatively and I hoped that the dolls would stimulate her curiosity and encourage her to play more freely.

I introduced two small pipe-cleaner figures, various pieces of dolls' house furniture and some other toys such as a car. The task was to play hide and seek 'in miniature' – play also being an important part of the task. Maria very quickly took on the imaginative play aspect, hide and seek was forgotten and her own games about families took over. More figures were found from the cupboard and elaborate stories began to unfold. The dolls' game became a metaphor through which she communicated her fears, thoughts, conflicts and anxieties. I think she expressed fears about who takes control when 'bad things happen'.

She also explored whether or not she could be acceptable as a child of mixed parentage and thought about where she belonged. In one session she looked through a basket full of miniature dolls saying 'Can we choose black ones?' Then she found another black baby and asking, 'Will it be OK if it is only a half caste?' gave it to me. As the weeks went on more and more black dolls were chosen until eventually the whole family was black.

Maria's stories revolved around a central theme of a wicked witch who came and stole babies. This story continued week after week and sometimes the mother and sometimes the police rescued the babies. The fear of children being snatched was very real for Maria. At her grandmother's funeral, her father had attempted to snatch her older sister. Her anxiety about 'who keeps babies safe' and 'what can be remembered' and 'what gets forgotten' was understandable. In her stories Maria was able to experience being controlled and being in control. Remembering the sequence of a story was generally difficult for her but through the games that she made up she was able to remember her story from the previous week, the names for all the characters and the exact position of the furniture. The exploration of difficult ideas about difference and loss, through her metaphor of the doll family was, I believe, helpful.

It was noticeable that after this period of play I had seen a big shift in the way that Maria said goodbye to her mother. She was now able to separate more easily, was less worried about her and more trusting of me. She seemed more relaxed and less watchful. During one game Maria was telling a bedtime story to the babies. It was – *'Once upon a time there was a little girl who went to play in the park. The wicked witch came and took her away. Her mum came and got her back and they all lived happily ever after.'* I likened her story to a fairy tale and this led us into our next term's work – The fairy story of *Hansel and Gretel*.

TERM 4 – HANSEL AND GRETEL

I chose to read *Hansel and Gretel* because it contained the themes of lost and found children, and wicked witch/stepmother who featured in Maria's stories. I also had several different editions of the story and was intending to read them all. All fairy tales have meaning and the meaning is different for each person and different for the same person at different times. I believed that reading this story several times and from different editions gave lots of opportunity to extract from it the meanings that were important to Maria. Bettelheim's book *The Uses of Enchantment*, lead me to hope that this story might be helpful. It might let her feel understood by me and help her to be more reflective. Maybe it would help her to make some sense of her inner turmoil and create a sense of order. Maria certainly had difficulty in organizing her thoughts, although outwardly she was practical and organized in her play.

Bettelheim (1976) says that 'the child is subject to desperate feelings of loneliness and isolation ... and often experiences mental anxiety. More often than not, he is unable to express these feelings in words'. He continues by saying that 'the need to be loved and the fear that one is thought worthless' are anxieties and dilemmas addressed directly in fairy tales.

When, towards the end of the third term, I began the stories of *Hansel and Gretel*, Maria at first just listened and made comments. In her choosing time she continued her games with the miniature dolls. The next weeks I read other editions of *Hansel and Gretel* and she still continued with her games. However, each week we would go over the story and she could remember some of the details. She became able to tell it back to me in a coherent way, she could remember which page we had ended on and would ask what words, like 'heavenly' meant. She made interesting remarks like 'the father looked terrified' and when reading the end of the second edition she said 'The stepmother died, perhaps she was the witch really because the witch had died in the oven, hadn't she?'

She also said 'I'd like to eat a piece of that gingerbread house'. Bettelheim (1976) says that, 'Hansel and Gretel, subjects of their own oral fixation, think nothing of eating the house that symbolically stands for the bad mother who has deserted them (forced them to leave home) and they do not hesitate to burn the witch to death in the oven as if it were food to be cooked for eating.' During one of the story readings Maria picked up two of the small figures and seemed to be enacting with them the illustrations in the book, but saying nothing.

Maria continued with her games but one week it took on a different feel. She was not the mother who fed and looked after her baby and 'got her back from witches' but a mother who became very cruel and punitive. In this game she pushed my baby away aggressively and the mother retaliated. She 'slapped her little girl on the face and made her stand with her face to the wall' then she put the dolls down saying she did not want to play with them any more. She appeared to be identifying with a rejecting mother at this point. She went to the cupboard (on her own!) and took out the puppets one by one. When she found the witch one she gasped loudly and said 'We could play

Hansel and Gretel.' She then continued to find other puppets to represent characters in the story but at this point did not want to continue. Perhaps it was too frightening and too real on that day.

The following week I created a 'Hansel and Gretel' board game. I left some opportunity for Maria to be able to add things to the games and to devise the rules. She added a longer pathway, houses, trees and a fire in the forest. We chose two small dolls each to be our Hansel and Gretel and a wicked witch that was positioned in the gingerbread house. We began to play. Rules were few and changed in the beginning because we were formulating them as we went along.

Landing on a witch's head meant that you had to go to the gingerbread house. Maria would move the witch threateningly along the path to get the children. She made up little conversations as she did, 'Right you children I'm going to get you and take you to my home, I'm going to keep you there', she said menacingly. She would get very excited and animated. She laughed and talked loudly, she flung her head back and put her head in her hands. When it came to her choosing time, she did not want to stop. At the end of a session she asked 'Can we play this next week?' We continued to play for the next nine weeks and we are still playing it at present as the educational psychotherapy continues.

There were unsettling times at home during this period but Maria continued to come week after week, looking forward to the games of 'Hansel and Gretel'. She made scoring sheets and she kept the score, letting me know regularly and accurately how many more times I had been to the witch's house than she had. This illustrated the fact that number was becoming meaningful. I think that through the 'Hansel and Gretel' game, Maria found a safe way of expressing her ambivalent and even hateful feelings towards her mother.

The witch symbolized the fear of things she didn't know. She did not like going to the witch's house when she landed on the witch's head square and found ways to avoid it such as cheating. She would say, 'It's scary and frightening and the witch is horrible'. When it was time to end the session, the end of the games had to be carefully considered. If you were in the witch's house it was a sad ending, if not, it was a happy one. Maria showed that she could tolerate both a happy and a sad end and that she was integrating both these aspects of herself.

During this period of time Maria had become more independent and exploratory (looking in cupboards) but was also experiencing me as a supportive person whom she could ask for help with 'school things'. She needed to learn to tell the time and she needed to know about speech marks. She wondered if I could help her with spellings and if we could make a book. Some time was given to these requests and by that time she was beginning to make real progress in school. Most of all, she was showing me that she was ready to take in what was being offered in the form of knowledge and learning.

Maria had continued being able to say goodbye to her mother in an age-appropriate way. In fact, although not an ideal arrangement, Maria waited for me alone in the waiting room and seemed happy to do so. Bettelheim (1976) says 'Hansel and Gretel deals with the difficulties and anxieties of the child who is forced to give up his dependent attachment to the mother and free himself of his oral fixation.' And

> Only by going out into the world can the fairy tale hero (the child) find himself there, and as he does he will also find the other with whom he will be able to live happily ever after, that is without ever again having to experience separation anxiety . . . to relinquish infantile dependency wishes and achieve a more satisfying existence.

Finally, it seems appropriate to quote, 'while it entertains the child, the fairy tale enlightens him about himself and fosters his personality development. It offers meaning on so many different levels and enriches the child's existence in so many ways.'

I think that through the use of the story of Hansel and Gretel, Maria was able to move on. It helped her to change from being someone who was compliant and needed to look after me to someone who was questioning and could be annoyed and cross when the game did not progress as she hoped. It fostered our relationship and in so doing she felt supported in her struggle to accept her own hateful and disappointed feelings. The story had been meaningful to her and had helped her to feel understood.

CONTACT WITH SCHOOL

I have already described my visit to Maria's new school where the head expressed her concerns about Maria's learning. I also heard about how, socially, Maria depended on her older sister in the playground and in class would not sit next to boys. However, the hardest thing to cope with, in the head and the class teacher's view, was this 'blanking off'. Her class teacher said 'She can't seem to do the simplest of tasks and sometimes it's as if she can't even speak.'

Maria joined a small special needs group and had extra help. I continued to visit each term and kept telephone contact with the head, particularly over missed sessions, making sure that we were all aware of any difficulties. Throughout the year Maria made good progress especially in reading where she went from level three up to level 10 on the school's reading scheme. Her special needs teacher reported that she was learning and remembering her weekly spellings and her writing became neat cursive script and more mature looking. She became able to tolerate sitting next to boys and ceased her dependency on her sister. However, Maria continued to 'blank off' or become 'stuck, frozen and almost paralysed' with anxiety in some situations. This remained an area of work to continue exploring at the clinic but the times when she did this became fewer. Teachers were pleased with her progress, and thought she was more confident and happy, less tense in school and more responsive.

At parents' evening at the end of the academic year, Ms O expressed to the head teacher how 'fed up she was at having to keep coming to the clinic'. It was not clear whether she meant for herself or for Maria but the head teacher explained to Ms O that attending the clinic sessions was important and had contributed to Maria's progress in school.

CONCLUSION

Maria was a little girl who lacked the confidence in her own thinking and had 'got stuck' in her relationships and her learning. Early experiences had resulted in an insecure relationship with her main attachment figures and this in turn affected her capacity to make use of adults in school and in the clinic. However she was able to explore past experiences and anxieties through play and tasks in a safe setting supported by a reliable adult.

I believe that Maria's preoccupation with thoughts and worries about loss and separation were, in part, what inhibited her progress in learning. Her 'switching off' and loss of concentration undoubtedly hindered her in school. At times during sessions when Maria was unable to communicate and seemed stuck and confused it was hard for me not to fill that empty space for her.

Other workers at the clinic had told me how unpredictable her mother could be. Maria needed to look after her mother, so she was always good and compliant. This too, was how she behaved when she first came to educational psychotherapy sessions. She seemed to wonder if she could be liked, if I would like her and what I would do if she were not good. Through the work in the sessions and through our developing trust these feelings were accepted.

Through the use of the small containing room, the contact I made with the teachers and the space made in our minds for thinking, Maria became freer to explore. She could think about the task and about herself more and think less of having to be 'nice' to me and look after me, so that I would like her. She was stronger and more robust and was able to walk around the room and look inside cupboards. She was able to bring feelings of sadness, disappointment and anger to the sessions as well as her affectionate and loving feelings.

The games using the miniature dolls and the board game of Hansel and Gretel were the metaphor that Maria could use to make sense of her own confusing and conflicting experiences. She came alive during these games and they freed her capacity to think. They allowed her to kill off the witches, or in other words her anxieties lessened and she understood that she could survive them. During the course of the educational psychotherapy, Maria regained her interest in learning and she made good progress at school.

COMMENTARY ON THE CASE STUDY OF MARIA

The case study of this girl was chosen because it allows the reader to see how the child, in educational psychotherapy, develops the capacity to learn and to relate to others with a maturity that had seemed unattainable at the beginning of the work.

In the normal course of development, a child learns to deal with separation during the latter part of the first year by experiencing it in a manageable way. Brief periods of being separated from the main caregiver are experienced as being tolerable because before the distress becomes too great, the child is again in touch with the adult. Children then use play to internalize the sense that separation can be borne and ultimately thought about. 'Peek-a-boo' and 'hide and seek' games are an important part of the learning experience as the child develops a sense of control over external events and a growing ability to deal with the anxiety associated with them.

In Maria's case, the traumatic experiences within the family made it difficult for this development to take place. She was, therefore, left with a feeling that she had to behave in a very attentive way to important adults and that any separation from them was potentially disastrous. She could not, therefore, think about anything other than her distress and did not have the emotional freedom to learn within the educational setting. Her therapist describes her reaction to being placed in an educational context:

> In the educational therapy room I invited Maria to have a look around. She found it difficult to go up to things, she glanced around, she stood close to her mother and at one point was touching her hair.

It is clearly important for Maria to be able to experience a relationship in which she becomes confident and from which she is then able to tolerate being parted. The educational psychotherapist uses a variety of metaphors both to understand what Maria is thinking about and to help her to experience different feelings. She begins by considering the picture drawn by Maria and notes that the picture full of happy, smiling faces and the girl's comment about angry feelings probably reflects her own experience. The therapist then recognizes that the end of the first term will be a difficult time for Maria and that careful preparation must be made, so that she can feel confident that the separation has been planned for and can be survived.

Books and games are important resources to offer the metaphorical experience of re-discovering what is temporarily lost. So the educational psychotherapist uses the *Where's Wally?* books and games of 'hide and seek' and 'Pelmanism' regularly to help the child to think about this in a manageable way. Subsequently, the use of dolls allows her to feel a greater sense of control over events. She is able to 'play' some of her anxieties and thoughts and to comment on things that are happening 'at one remove' from herself and are therefore more tolerable. Some of the play gives the educational psychotherapist an indication that the use of a fairy story may be another very important source of learning for Maria. The child refers, in a story she tells the dolls, to a 'wicked witch' who came and took her away. Her therapist likens this to the story of *Hansel and Gretel* and uses that as a basis for further educational tasks.

A number of editions of the story are used so that the story is repeated but in varying forms. Gradually, by using the doll play, Maria was able to express some of her thoughts about the mother figure being not only a nurturing and caring ideal but also someone who can be experienced as cruel and unfeeling. At first, this thought, even in the metaphor, is quite frightening for Maria, but she is able to come back to it in her use of puppets and the board game and to express by these means, the ambivalent and even hateful feelings she may have about important figures in her life.

This is a child who does not give obvious clues to her needs. Her head teacher asks the educational psychotherapist 'What are we going to do with her?' and describes her as a 'brick wall', a 'typical daydreamer'. A child who deals with her difficulties in this way is just as confusing as one who acts out her anger and distress because she appears to create a barrier between herself and others and between herself and the learning task. The educational psychotherapist has to be very alert to any indication the child gives of what her internal world is like. She then has to choose carefully the tools that the child will be able to use to internalize a less inhibiting set of defences. In doing this, Maria is helped to relate not only to her therapist and the tasks they enjoy together but also to transfer some of what she has learned to both school and family relationships.

A child who may be described as a 'resistant anxiously attached child' like Maria might need a teacher to be very proactive in making a relationship with her and to challenge her belief that she is unwanted or unappreciated. Occasional one-to-one time with her while an assistant takes the class would be valuable if practicable.

A class teacher might also note Maria's good capacity to use opportunities to write and draw about the thoughts and worries that preoccupy her and she might choose curriculum activities and themes relevant to her preoccupations. Because of Maria's experience of losses and abrupt endings, she might benefit from careful preparation for school breaks or new teachers. Learning through classroom games that involve the expression of hostility may also be helpful.

5 Ethical Considerations When Working Psychotherapeutically with Children

The authors take the view that there is a general consensus among professionals about the areas covered in taking an ethical approach and consider some of the practical issues that arise when working psychotherapeutically with children. There cannot be a model for dealing with each situation but there can be an internal set of guidelines for planning good practice.

Most professions working with either children or adults have devised codes of practice that aim to protect both workers and their clients. This is because it is recognized that, in the intimacy of the relationship between the two, it is possible for thoughts and actions to occur that can damage one or both of the parties. It is also the case that there are many external influences on the work such as the concerns of parents and teachers, the prevalent attitudes of society and the economic context. To have a framework within which to make decisions regarding the conduct of individual work, both within and outside the sessions allows much clearer thinking about the issues to be taken into consideration and the risks that can appropriately be taken.

TEACHERS'/EDUCATIONAL PSYCHOTHERAPISTS' OWN FEELINGS AFFECTING THEIR WORK

Educational psychotherapists are required to have an extended period of personal psychoanalytic psychotherapy during their training. This is to enable therapists to consider elements in their own way of thinking that may affect the work and to bring these features into consciousness. But, as many teachers or other workers find, it is possible to have very strong feelings about a child or a group of children with whom you are working, and to be unaware of the source of the experience. There follow some examples of the way in which this can affect the work.

Paul was working with a child with whom he identified rather strongly. He felt that the child physically resembled him and this led him to understand the child's needs in terms of his own remembered experience. It became difficult for him to interpret the child's behaviour or understand the child's creative work in terms that were free of his subjective feelings until he was able to recognize what was happening and acknowledge that this child's internal world might be different from his own.

Lindsay was working with a lively and creative boy whose mother struggled to meet her own needs together with those of her son. The mother found it difficult to bring her son for the regular sessions that had been arranged when her own employment took precedence. There were reports that she often left the boy with relatives at weekends when she had other social commitments. It was difficult for Lindsay to separate her work with the child from her very critical view of the mother, her rivalrous feelings towards her and her sympathy for the child. This led her, at times, to encourage the child to express his annoyance about things that had happened in relation to his mother rather than allowing a re-experiencing of his angry feelings within the psychotherapeutic relationship.

In these cases, the therapists were already engaged in regular supervision of their clinical sessions and thus had the opportunity of thinking about what was happening. Most of those who work with individual children are not automatically receiving clinical supervision but can be alerted to the need of it by the fact that they wish to talk to colleagues about the children they see. Discussion within an appropriate professional framework is an important part of any work and particularly with that concerning children. Clinical supervision offers a perspective on the emotional issues surrounding psychotherapeutic education. If it is not made automatically available by the institutional framework within which the work is being carried out, it is important to consider how a support system can be set up.

THINKING ABOUT WHAT YOU ARE DOING

Many teachers and others who work with children who have learning or behavioural difficulties find that the children lack the capacity to think and that 'not knowing' something is such a painful experience for them that they have to find ways of evading such a situation. The adult worker has developed the capacity to think by building on the very early experiences of tolerating a degree of frustration. There are times, however, when the work throws up possibilities that are experienced as so confusing or difficult that it is preferable to evade them. Wondering why children behave in particular ways or why they do not appear to learn what we teach can be very puzzling and may lead us to grasp a 'diagnosis' that seems to give an answer to our questions. Both parents and professionals can see a diagnosis as having a very 'containing' function and can welcome the certainty it appears to bring to the child's needs. Working therapeutically with a child, however, also requires the capacity to keep an open mind about the nature of his learning or behavioural problems, to form hypotheses and revise these as the child's responses and difficulties becomes clearer.

Educational psychotherapists make a written record of what has happened in a session or any meeting or incident in which they have been involved. An account of the process of the interaction allows the possibility of thinking about what has happened and the meaning of both the child's and the therapist's own contribution to it. The records are a particularly useful resource during supervision sessions. They may not be the permanently kept records of the work but are some of the tools of a 'reflective practitioner'. Thought also needs to be given to the way in which a permanent record is kept and the therapist should bear in mind the agreed usual practice of a clinic, school or other institution.

DEALING WITH VIOLENCE

Some of the most difficult children in school are those who have the most tenuous connection with their teachers or their peer group. Children who have, in early life, been unable to make an attachment because they have not experienced an adult who is able to be attuned to them often have no concept of boundaries and do not easily feel supported by them. Working with a child who does not appear to respect the institution or the people in it can initially feel very threatening. To be able to talk calmly and to listen without reacting in a hostile way can be regarded as a psychotherapeutic tool. So also can the maintenance of the safety of all concerned by ensuring that the work takes place within a school or clinic where there are other adults nearby so that child and worker do not have to cope with a frightening sense of isolation.

If there seems a real possibility that the child may act out some violent feelings by attacking the contents of the room or the adult it is important to make clear that this is not acceptable. The therapist or teacher needs to have thought out some strategy for dealing with this potentially difficult situation as it is not helpful to have to intervene physically unless someone is otherwise at significant risk of harm. If another adult can be made available to take the child into a safe space it becomes possible to end the session so that work can be resumed the following week without a breakdown of the relationship. An angry attack on the child's 'violence' and an exclusion from the school as a whole is less helpful because it implies that the adults are overwhelmed by the child's angry feelings and cannot 'contain' them.

It can sometimes come as a relief if a particularly difficult child is absent from school. There is a temptation to ignore the absence and fail to put into action any procedure that would return the child to the school. Some schools choose to 'reward' failure to attend by exclusion.

THINKING ABOUT ABSENCE

In the case of Kevin, there is a period when absences occur and his educational psychotherapist is able to link this in her mind with the unsettled feeling among her co-workers and the difficulty for all the adults, of holding his needs in mind. Educational psychotherapists, working in a clinical setting, make a practice of acknowledging an unplanned absence by sending a small note to keep the link between the previous session and the next one, and to help the child to know that he or she remains in the therapist's mind. When the child next attends a session the therapist will be alert to the possibility that the child will act out some anger towards her for the missed session (regardless of the fact that she was not responsible for it). Any sense of injustice that the therapist feels about this will be helpful in understanding the transferred feelings that the child is unconsciously communicating. She will put into words the anger the child may feel towards her and may speak of how difficult it is for the child to be sure that she can think of the child when the child is not there. This helps children to realize that the turmoil they feel is something that can be thought about and 'contained'.

A teacher working individually with a child in school has to make a judgement about the level of personal relationship that has been developed. If the work regularly takes place and is part of a psychotherapeutic intervention, it is important to recognize that making it meaningful to the child can have an effect on his capacity to learn. Some symbolic way of recognizing the link, such as giving the child a note to bring back at the beginning of the following term after a holiday break, can perform a similar function to the note sent after an unexpected break. If this does not seem appropriate it is important to ensure that the absence has been followed up – checking to see that it has been verified by the parent and following it up with a school secretary's or attendance officer's telephone call if it has not.

AREA OF COMPETENCE

The way that an educational psychotherapist working in clinical or school setting would practise differs somewhat from the way in which a teacher working individually with a child in school might work. It is very helpful to recognize the subtle differences of practice that make the work therapeutic but does not constitute 'psychotherapy'. It is considered ethically sound to remain within one's area of competence and both child and adult gain considerable benefit from the process that the adult goes through when thinking about what is appropriate practice. This can be achieved by reading accounts of others' work and from studying the underlying meaning that can be found in the behaviour and language of both adult and child. Because of the way in which workers can be affected by some of the children, it is important to do much of the thinking separately from the child. Then the response to the child can use the unconscious influences as part of the understanding rather than being an impediment to it.

Working psychotherapeutically and being in touch with a child's emotional state sometimes makes therapists aware of aspects of the child's mental state that are beyond their competence to deal with and need to be referred to another professional. This might include a child who is self-harming or who experiences suicidal thoughts. There is also reference below to other protocols regarding, for example, disclosures of sexual or physical abuse that require contact with other professionals. The therapist will have made clear to the child at the very beginning of the work that the sessions will be confidential but that if the child is thought to be in any danger it may be necessary to share that information with another adult.

PHYSICAL CONTACT

There is a time, in the work with Kevin, when his educational psychotherapist relates how he is reluctant to end the session and asks her to push him round in the chair. She experienced something like 'rocking a rather large baby in a pram' as he lay back and gazed up at the ceiling with a soporific grin on his face. She recognizes that, at this point, Kevin has a great wish to have the experience of being a baby who is being held and responded to by a maternal figure who can understand what his needs currently are. He has initiated this because he does not want to end the session and, in a defensive strategy to avoid the pain of ending, chooses to revert to a baby stage.

Part of the therapeutic process is to re-experience some period when development was adversely affected in the more manageable context of the psychotherapeutic environment. When children begin to feel, unconsciously, that this opportunity presents itself, they may seek an opportunity to 'regress' to an earlier stage and may wish to be 'tucked up' in a chair or on a couch, or may seem to want to be cuddled. It is helpful to think of ways in which a nurturing experience can be offered while retaining an appropriate boundary. This might include reading a story to a child, rather than asking the child to share in the reading. It may also involve sharing in the making of a model or some other cooperative activity. This can then lead on to the possibility of greater playfulness in a more competitive activity such as playing a game. Maria's educational psychotherapist reflects on the description of Maria as a 'brick wall' and the need for her to experience adult 'reverie' in order to play and then to learn.

CREATING A SAFE ENVIRONMENT

For children who have been involved in very damaging relationships or experiences in the past and who have not been able to deal with them in a way that allows them to think objectively about them, there is the possibility that something within the therapy can excite a reawakening of the earlier experience. It is very important to give the child a feeling of safety, and this can be encouraged by the structure of the work. Regular times and rooms that are predictable and appropriate, help to give a sense of containment. Some institutions, such as schools, are not accustomed to providing a private space for individual work because education is usually practised as a communal activity and does not have the personal focus of a therapeutic approach. Trying to preserve a private space for a therapeutic relationship between two people can excite curiosity on the part of other adults and children and make the space very vulnerable to encroachment. The therapist has to think about ways of preserving the privacy.

The educational psychotherapist also has to be aware that there are choices to be made about which children may benefit from a therapeutic approach. This does not imply that a successful intervention can be guaranteed but that, as mentioned earlier in the book, for some children, close contact with a personally thoughtful mind can be very tantalizing. It can lead to a troubling feeling of conflict and sense of disloyalty for the child if comparisons are made with other significant adults. In her work with Kevin, his therapist writes of the 'demanding and at times difficult' nature of the work. He is able to gain from the therapy despite the contrast between her thoughtfulness and the unreliability of some of the adults caring for him.

There are some children, however, whose situation is so unsafe that the experience of individual work of this type would not be suitable. To a child who may be experiencing ongoing physical abuse or is being emotionally abused or made a scapegoat, the setting up of the educational psychotherapy may demonstrate collusion with the abuse and the potential for further damage. It would also be as inappropriate for therapists to work with the child of parents with whom they had a social relationship as it would for psychologists to carry out assessments of their own children. In these cases, there is confusion about the relationship with the client, which can lead to a violation of trust.

It becomes clear, at times, that a child already in therapy is being abused. Children's drawings or stories may give a clue to this, or their growing trust in the therapist may allow some more direct revelation of what is happening. When the therapy is starting the therapist will have made clear to the child what the 'rules of engagement' are. These will include a statement that the child will not be allowed to hurt himself or her, or damage the room or equipment irreparably. It will also have been made clear that although the content of the sessions is confidential to the two of them, the therapist may have to inform others if the child seems to be in some danger. If it becomes clear that the child is engaging in sexual activity or is being abused there are very clear guidelines laid down about the reporting of such information. It is essential that any worker is conversant with protocols and that the appropriate procedures are followed.

A school or clinic should also have protocols for recording occasions when children have been at risk if, for example, they have run out of the room, inadvertently hurt themselves, required physical restraint or have become inconsolably upset. It may be that an incident report should be written up, or a manager informed and the child needs to be aware of this. This can form part of the structure that helps a child to feel safe. Networks of adults involved with a child try to practise transparency by sending copies of letters to clients and by including parents and children in meetings. There is a balance to be maintained between being open in informing all concerned and preserving confidentiality.

At times, despite a worker's best endeavours, difficulties can arise that are hard to 'contain'. One child psychotherapist (Ironside, 1995) wrote movingly about the experience of having a false allegation of sexual abuse made against a worker and the effect on both the worker and the child of the procedures for dealing with such an allegation. He also cites three other examples of work with children who made allegations that were managed within the very close network of professionals that had been built up and where the psychotherapy was able to bring about some progress in the children's capacity to make relationships. These examples and the ethical codes we work by, remind therapists and others who do individual work with children, of the need to remain within the limits of their competence and to seek regular consultation about their work with senior colleagues.

CONFIDENTIALITY

The parents and other professionals involved with a child may perceive teachers or therapists as very powerful people even though they may not feel this themselves. They may seem to exercise power by withholding information, by understanding or not understanding, by setting boundaries or by being a figure in whom are located many transferred feelings. Because of this the therapist has to find ways of keeping the network informed while being sensitive to the confidential information to which she is party. It is important to make a distinction between confidentiality and secrecy.

When consideration of the work is taken outside the professional network directly involved, for instance if the work is used for research, the client should be asked to give permission. All identifying details should be changed.

6 Case Study of Tariq, A Child Persecuted by Destructive Phantasies

This case study, written by Patricia Reid, describes work with a boy whose behaviour resembles that of a traumatized or disorganized child. In an attempt to manage extreme anxiety Tariq, a year 1 boy, projects feelings such as aggression into imagined things or people. He then fears retaliation from the world of monsters he has created. As a consequence there is little space in his head for learning.

The main challenge to his educational psychotherapist is to demonstrate that she can remain benign and thoughtful despite his attacking behaviour. Over time her capacity to 'contain' his anxiety allows him to own some of the negative feelings that he previously projected into others. He is then able to be more in touch with feelings such as sadness and remorse. He begins to acknowledge and internalize a helpful, benign adult and as his anxiety diminishes 'space' is made for learning tasks.

INTRODUCTION, FAMILY BACKGROUND AND SCHOOL SITUATION

Tariq's family was referred to the Child and Adolescent Mental Health Services (CAMHS) clinic during the summer when Tariq was in year 1 of his primary school. His mother and father had come over several years before from Egypt for fertility treatment. The twins, Tariq and his brother, were born after several IVF attempts and the parents continued to be seen by their GP and the child development clinic after their birth. As the children entered their second year the parents found managing them increasingly difficult. The twins were described by their parents as aggressive, uncooperative, overly rivalrous and murderous towards each other and sometimes towards their father. There were also major concerns about Tariq soiling himself at home and school and hiding the stools.

Tariq's mother was suffering from chronic depression and his father had a kidney problem. At times they felt overwhelmed and defeated by the children's needs. Both parents were under the care of the hospital. They were living in very cramped conditions, were relying on financial support from Egypt and had enormous concerns about the implications of returning to their country of origin while they felt they needed continuing health care for themselves and support in caring for the twins. There was also the question of whether the parents would remain in the United Kingdom in order to have further fertility treatment.

During May, when in the reception class, the school arranged for the educational psychologist to observe Tariq. His teachers were extremely concerned about his lack of academic progress and his increasingly bizarre, aggressive and unmanageable behaviour and encopresis. More than once the school had come close to excluding him. The educational psychologist concluded that Tariq might be suffering from expressive language delay, durational attention and concentration difficulties and that these together with emotional and behavioural difficulties were affecting his ability to learn. Following the educational psychologist's involvement, a case conference was organized at the school to discuss which agency would best meet the needs of the family and to begin the process of applying for a statement of special educational needs. At this time it was also arranged that they would see the family therapist at the CAMHS clinic with a view to encouraging more positive parenting and to provide strategies for the management of Tariq's encopresis and general behaviour. A series of appointments was made throughout that year and the following one and the parents and children attended regularly. Attempts to regulate Tariq's encopresis using behavioural strategies and the 'sneaky poo' game failed.

Eventually it was recommended that Tariq have an individual assessment session with the consultant child psychotherapist. She suggested that Tariq was experiencing developmental delay, that his thought processes were disordered but that it was difficult to be more specific than this until the possibility of any organic reason for his difficulties had been investigated. He was referred to the consultant community paediatrician, who concluded that there was no evidence of neurological deterioration or specific neurological abnormality and that the history of his encopresis strongly suggested an emotional and behavioural basis. Following this consultation and other discussions with the consultant child psychotherapist and the consultant psychologist, the possibility arose that Tariq would be suitable as my second educational psychotherapy training case.

Appointments were arranged for the following Spring term, with me, the family therapist, Tariq's parents and Tariq and his twin brother. During the initial meeting with the two children and parents, they described Tariq as experiencing night terrors, having 'a madness of his mind', and generally being unmanageable, aggressive and overwhelmingly difficult to control. He would not do any homework and persistently denied that he soiled. It was also reported at the meeting that a speech therapist had described him as experiencing semantic pragmatic disorder. The consultant paediatrician thought of ADHD.

SESSIONS IN SPRING AND SUMMER: TERMS 1 AND 2

Tariq is a chunky boy, bordering on the chubby. He is tall for his age with a mass of thick dark hair, enormous brown eyes and long eyelashes. His chubby cheeks and hands and rounded belly gave him the singular appearance of an oversized baby. His walk was ungainly and flatfooted. He presented as a bright, alert, quizzical child and when he played with small toys or held writing implements his reported poor gross motor skills were not immediately apparent. I learned from Tariq's mother that he had just begun to take Ritalin at the beginning of the term.

I was able to administer reading and spelling assessments and complete the Raven's Coloured Matrices with Tariq. His reading age scored at below six years and his spelling age at below five years. On the Raven, Tariq scored at above average in underlying nonverbal ability. He was uncooperative about simple number sequencing tasks and appeared to have no number skills beyond recognizing groups of two and three objects.

TARIQ'S MONSTERS

During these early sessions Tariq drew and painted many monsters, which were all very large and filled A2 sheets of sugar paper. He used bold colours, blue, black, red, white and a wide variety of shapes; dinosaurs, flying birds, long snakes. They were all outlined in black paint. When we played the squiggle game Tariq turned all my squiggles into monsters. Enquiries from me about his drawings were often greeted with comments that had an emphasis on an oral phantasy of eating or being eaten; 'it will eat you up', 'shut up' or 'I will squirt this at you' (paint) or resolute silence. Sometimes he would be more forthcoming – one particular monster would 'eat you up at night. You have to find a safe hiding place. Not in the bushes – he can hear you move. Not under the bed because he can feel you. It's very fast; it runs faster than any other creature.' It seemed that there was no escape for Tariq from these persecuting, determined demons. I wondered if he felt scared being with me and wanted to hide from me but on reflection his monster output was so prolific and all his solitary play with the toy animals so aggressive and destructive that I wondered if this was his narrative for letting me know just how bad and scary everything was for him and how full he was of these monsters. I wondered, too, about his being full with dangerous poo that could be expelled at any time of the day.

When thinking about Tariq and these monsters and his encopresis it is useful to consider Kleinian theory and its description of the paranoid/schizoid position. The individual who has never completely left the paranoid/schizoid position behind can split the good and bad internal experiences and then, being unable to tolerate the bad, project them out into external objects. However, the bad internal objects are not completely diminished by this functioning and the individual's 'central anxiety then becomes a fear of being attacked and overwhelmed by hostile internal and external forces' (Klein, 1975).

> In phantasy the child's faeces can become attacking objects and can be involved in sadistic phantasies whose number, variety and richness are all but inexhaustible.

If Tariq was involved in employing primitive defences (splitting and projection) to an extreme degree in order to keep the bad away, it was, perhaps, little wonder that he had limited mental and emotional space left within him for paying attention and learning at school. This would be especially so if he was vulnerable to his attacking poos invading his activities at any time, which seemed to be the case; there was no reported pattern to his soiling.

At the end of the sessions he liked to be in control of how his pictures were stored. He paid close attention to order and cleanliness. This was in marked contrast to his messy, uncontrollable soiling and stool hiding and possibly the defence mechanism named by Freud as reaction formation. At the end of other sessions he complained about the condition of his cupboard: 'it is dirty'. This felt like an angry, dismissive criticism of me and an example of projective identification, that I too was bad, dirty and useless in the fight against monsters and attacking poo.

TARIQ'S PLAY WITH ANIMALS AND FIGURES

When Tariq played with the small figures and animals they danced, fell to the floor, charged at, attacked, maimed, chased away and destroyed one another. Animals and dinosaurs constantly fell injured to the floor and lay forgotten. The play with these toys felt chaotic and uncontained and despite overt aggression towards me, I felt that I should not interrupt his narrative with too many comments. He did not invite my participation in this play and it seemed that it was my function to watch, to take it in and not be overwhelmed by it and never to retaliate. My role was to contain his frustration and aggression, just as the maternal object needs to take in and contain the infant's excessive and frightening anxieties, reflect upon them and return them in a more manageable form (Bion, 1962a, 1962b).

Bion describes this function of the maternal figure, containing the unbearable for the infant, as being the precursor to the formation of a mental apparatus for thinking. If Tariq was still seeking someone to contain his overwhelming infantile anxieties then perhaps he had not yet acquired a good-enough ability to think. This would help explain his inattention, hyperactive and 'thoughtless' behaviour at school.

TARIQ AND PERSECUTING EYES

Tariq would often go for my eyes with sharp objects such as a small toy snake, pencils or paintbrushes. When he became more able to look at books, he became preoccupied with illustrations of peering eyes. Somewhere there was a possible persecutory phantasy about eyes and being watched. I felt there was a connection between being watched and 'not feeling known' or dropped from mind as the animals and figures were dropped during play.

One of the infant's earliest experiences is being taken in and held in mind by the way the mother looks at him during those moments of wordless communication between mother and baby. It is important, in these moments that the infant's feelings and anxieties are recognized. Perhaps Tariq was experiencing not being held in mind, or seen as he really was. For Tariq, feeling watched or looked at was not experienced as an effort at healthy containment and understanding but as the projection of persecutory and dangerous phantasies.

ERRATIC ATTENDANCE AND FEELINGS OF DEFEAT

The later Spring Term sessions were characterized by nonattendance, by Tariq and his mother often arriving late or his mother repeatedly asking if the session time could be changed. One session when they arrived 25 minutes late and when Tariq was in my room I noticed that he had brought a smell with him. But I lacked experience and was not sure of my senses and I said nothing. It was only during a subsequent meeting with the family therapist that the mother confirmed that Tariq had soiled on this occasion. It was the only time he soiled with me.

During some sessions Tariq employed omnipotent, bossy dismissal of any activity I offered. I wondered about him feeling so overwhelmed and defeated by his own frightening preoccupations that hopelessness spilled out into the surrounding agencies that were trying to help, much as Tariq's poos spilled out into his pants. This sense of defeat invaded the school staff as they reported that they felt overwhelmed and powerless to help Tariq's mother when he threw himself into a rage and refused to comply with her requests. This sense of defeat seemed to invade my attempts at encouraging him to look at words and learn about written language.

It was important that I maintained the sessions' boundaries and had the room set out in the same way and at the same time each week. I was not to give up or be harmed by Tariq's aggressive impulses and had to return unscathed the following week. It was reported by the family therapist that the parents had had a defeated attitude towards the behavioural approach in helping with his encopresis, the sneaky-poo game. Tariq was the only one to remember it.

IDEALIZATION

When Tariq was asked to draw a picture of his family doing something together they liked or often did, Tariq drew a picture of himself and his mother and no one else. The figures were well executed but of equal size and were floating above the ground. He coloured in the figures, his mother all in black, and he added a blue sky and completed his picture with a shining sun in the corner. He was intense and careful throughout the production of this picture and fully absorbed in it. When I enquired about other family members he remained silent and intent on the drawing. On reflection, the figures looked as if they were running away. They were leaning in the same direction, mirroring each other, their feet 'not touching the ground'. This spontaneous drawing hints at Tariq's close identification with his mother and his concern for her, which she has reported to the family therapist, saying 'he always worries about me and I don't know why'.

When rejoining his mother at the end of sessions. Tariq was always very affectionate towards her. There was no inhibition in his desire to touch and cuddle her. Anna Freud describes bodily products, when surrendered to the mother during the potty-training phase, as being highly cathected with libido and therefore also with strong feelings of love and hate. 'The toddler's entire attitude towards the object world is dominated by violent swings between love and hate.' In the paranoid-schizoid position, in which Tariq was possibly stuck, the chief defences are splitting, projective identification and idealization. These defences have a powerful effect on thinking (Klein, 1975). Tariq seemed full of hate in his sessions with me and then overwhelmed with tender feelings towards his mother. If he was still stuck in infantile splitting then this would perhaps contribute to his reported developmental delay; toddlers, after all, cannot read and write.

THE LEARNING TASKS

In these early sessions, beyond writing his name on two A4 exercise books, Tariq would not participate in any word games or activities and would not look at any reading books. He did not initially take up my offer of reading to him. I would always persist with the offer of these reading and writing activities but they were received with contemptuous dismissal. His anxiety and resistance in connection with looking at and attempting to read words meant that I could not help him learn anything. On one occasion when a reading task was offered Tariq said that he 'did not want to let the words out' as if they, too, were in danger of becoming attacking objects. I felt out of control of the situation, dominated by Tariq's threats and his fear. He appeared to keep me locked out of any relationship with him by not looking at me, appearing not to listen to things that I said or rudely complaining that my voice was a nuisance to him. He was strongly defended against having anything 'pushed'.

Looking back and rereading the session notes, it seems as if, because Tariq wanted and/or needed to keep me out of this scary world, I was kept defensively at a distance. I wondered if he needed to keep me separate from his frightening inner world populated with destructive monsters. And while he appeared to hate being in the room with me he also needed to keep me uncontaminated and not participating – as if he had a story to tell and did not wish to be interrupted in the telling; to leave his horrors with me and to have me return unharmed the next week. I wonder now if his dislike and difficulty in returning each week was to do with fearing what damage he might have done to me and what retaliation awaited him (Klein, 1975).

FURTHER LEARNING ACTIVITIES AND SMALL CHANGES

During the later sessions of the Summer Term, Tariq began very tentatively to take an interest in the books arranged around the room. Some of the session time was not being filled up with Tariq's monsters and room was made for reading. The books he chose for me to read to him over and over were *Where the Wild Things Are* and the Tom and Pippo books. *Where the Wild Things Are* is the story about a small boy who, having been told off by his mother, dreams or fantasizes about a journey to the land of monsters. He then becomes king of the monsters and tames them. The Tom and Pippo books are about the relationship between a small boy and his father. They are short books with simple realistic illustrations. In the first book, Tom is reprimanded by his father for making a mess. Tom copes with this reprimand by then telling off his toy monkey, Pippo. I asked Tariq how he thought Tom might be feeling and he said 'sad – no angry, very angry'. It appeared to be a moment when a painfully sad feeling was allowed a momentary airing before becoming quickly masked by the defence of anger. It felt like a small movement in the work. Sadness could exist side by side with anger. At the end of *Where the Wild Things Are*, I commented that the mother had left the boy something to eat and drink after his long journey with monsters. Tariq slumped back in his chair and was quiet. Again it felt like a moment when reparative, tender feelings and disappointment could exist alongside monsters and cross daddies and mummies.

After this exchange, Tariq curled himself up in a foetal position under the desk and I commented on how small he had suddenly become and, as if feeling his own vulnerability, he quickly jumped up and wanted to attack me with a pencil. Then play involving attacking monsters began again. This time they were ones that come at night and hide up his nose. He jammed the pencil into the mouth of the crocodile. Again his sadistic phantasies are penetrating the openings of his body and persecuting him with bad smells. Tariq, it seemed, could not bear to feel small and dependent. This would explain why he defended against this feeling by appearing bossy and omnipotent.

During the Summer term I always had simple CVC and CCVC word tasks available, usually matching and colouring, or sequencing. Their place in the sessions was limited as Tariq's initial preoccupations were with settling the monsters in the room and in our relationship. But he became more willing to have me read to him and to study the books. Following the repeated reading of the Tom and Pippo books, one session Tariq decided to repair the cup and tea pot he had made for his mother some time back in the spring term and which had fallen apart during the drying process. He asked for my help with this task, which again felt like an acknowledgement that he and I could work together, that I was not quite such a useless ally. At the end of this session Tariq painted a ghost. He called it a 'gooney ghost'. It was an amorphous shape in pale whispy colours. It was not scary and I wondered if his monsters were becoming more ghostlike and less fierce. These small changes could indicate a movement towards the Kleinian depressive position. The infant's concern shifts from a preoccupation with the survival of self to a concern for the object upon which he or she depends. One of the consequences of this shift is the emergence of reparative capacities (Klein, 1975).

The end of the work of the Summer term came rather abruptly, on 5 June, so at least six weeks before the end of the term. Tariq's mother brought him to the clinic and said that they were going to Egypt until September. They had been granted leave to remain in Britain and so could now come and go as they pleased. Unexpectedly, then, this was to be Tariq's last session for 12 weeks. When I went to the waiting room he was underneath a chair and refusing to come out. His mum tried admonishments in Arabic and pulling him, all to no avail. I suggested he came to help me put away his things for the summer and he complied. Once in the room Tariq picked up a few books one by one and jammed them carelessly into the cupboard. He said he was leaving and headed for the door. It seemed that ending was so painful that he needed to get it over with quickly. I picked up a paintbrush and began using some red paint. Tariq stopped and took over. He spent the remainder of the session producing three enormous ferocious monsters on A1 sheets of paper. If I asked him anything about them he grunted or ignored me. He asked for no help with pouring paint in the trays or cleaning the brushes. I felt he wanted to show me that he did not need me and that his monsters were an expression of how angry he felt. The only moment when he dropped his defence against the feelings about this sudden ending was when he asked what would happen to his pictures. I said they would be safe, and showed him where I would keep them until September. As he left the room at the end he said, 'you need to wipe your walls' (there were unshiftable old paint stains on them). This was my first experience of an ending and it had come without any preparation. It is apparent, now, that Tariq was telling me that he didn't need me, that he was very angry with me that he was leaving me with his angry monsterish feelings. He left, remarking dismissively on how unpleasant and dirty my room was anyway. He was, therefore, not going to miss it.

AUTUMN AND SPRING: TERMS 3 AND 4 AND FURTHER SMALL CHANGES

Tariq's statement of special educational needs had come through. He now had 25 hours of one-to-one support from a classroom assistant and three hours of one-to-one literacy support. The school also reported that he was no longer taking Ritalin. Tariq returned to the clinic for one last session before the work was transferred to the school premises. His mother and father were full of despair again about bringing him to his appointments and the school felt helpless to support them. After discussions with the school and a room at school being made available, the transfer was conducted smoothly, with only the smallest protest of disgust from Tariq. But, the first session when we played the squiggle game, my squiggle for Tariq was turned into a large, complex swirling maze with two small boys trapped in the middle and a monster breaking through the perimeter. I wondered if I was the monster breaking into his world at school and if he felt angry with me for coming. His response to this was to draw an ugly round face with glasses and its tongue poking out. Tariq said this was me.

When we started our work again after the summer and Christmas breaks, Tariq displayed his continued contempt for me by criticizing the books and activities and engaging in more fighting between the dinosaurs and larger jungle animals; bottoms and willies were bitten ferociously. During the spring term the aggressive play turned to the small toy people who were systematically drowned, eaten, soiled with brown paint, covered in 'pepper' and buried under quantities of PVA glue. He tutted when a paint brush broke after some rough treatment and I wondered if he was criticizing me for having broken the work through a break. He used a pencil and drove it towards his eye and into his mouth and I wondered about how angry he was feeling towards me. He was rude and sullen and would ask me what 'arse fucking' meant. My squiggles were not 'good enough' and he would 'test' my competence by asking me questions about times tables and how far he could go in provoking me. It was a testing time in the sessions and important that I remained able to take up all his anger and disgust without pushing it back. The books brought the opportunity for shared reading and as the weeks passed each term he would pick up this activity where it had been left.

He asked me to read *The Monster Bed* (a story about a baby monster with bedtime anxieties who would attack his mother). This book and *The Selfish Crocodile* (a story about a large ugly crocodile who will not share its river) became his favourites over the next few months and I had to read them over and over again. The re-reading of books with a theme significant to the child's emotional inner world can help the child experience negative and hostile feelings and provide a means of communicating them to someone else (Caspari, 1980). Whenever I read to Tariq I had the strongest urge to protect the silent reverie he would fall into while looking at the book; I felt that I should not read too quickly or turn the pages too suddenly – that I must not startle him.

These moments felt soothing and calming, a moment when Tariq's hostile feelings could be given expression and taken up by me (Winnicott, 1971a, 1971b). He liked to count the monster eyes hidden in the forest trees and I talked about how it must feel scary to feel watched all the time. He continued to act out destructive, sadistic attacks using the dinosaurs and to ask for the same books to be read. His play remained a solitary narrative acted out with me as a silent and benign audience. When this activity had exhausted him he would often make something from the clay, a vase, more pots, a horse, a small boy.

Gradually the educational content was given a place and I began lots of word recognition and pairing tasks using large monsters covered in words. Tariq accepted these activities as long as they did not involve him in any writing. As Tariq read or paired sight words or CVC or simple CCVC words he was allowed to paint in a section of the beast. Over the weeks, this way of managing educational tasks was accepted and relished by Tariq. He made a large collection of these painted word creatures and one day I was able to suggest he wrote a story using them. I could not have predicted Tariq's enthusiasm for this task and he set about folding sugar paper and asking for my help in stapling them together so that they formed a book. He painted the cover of his 'book' silver and wrote: 'Tariq and aninal fun' on the cover. He asked for the spelling of animal only and obviously misheard the *m* for an *n*. In the event Tariq dictated two stories.

From this work I experimented with the introduction of other methods of encour- aging Tariq's growing ability to look at words. I met with success and failure in equal proportions. Tasks that worked well were ones where Tariq could feel like an active participant in a game. Tasks that seemed less acceptable were ones that bore any resemblance to school worksheets. One task that was well received involved Tariq climbing steps with each word read successfully. Into this task he introduced his team. Tariq read and therefore climbed the steps before the other two. At the end of this task Tariq engaged in an elaborate award ceremony with him standing on the podium bearing the title '1st Place'. For Tariq, learning is tightly bound with winning and losing; it is a forceful competition and failure means disaster and coming 'last'. It is not difficult then to understand why Tariq found it difficult to place himself in the position of 'not knowing', of being last and then finding it difficult to take small steps in acquiring literacy skills and risk making mistakes. In a safe relationship with me, Tariq could risk making mistakes and also act out his phantasies of coming first. Irene Caspari (1980) describes how enabling a child to succeed or to 'win' at a learning task allows the child to experience rivalrous competitive emotions, which may contribute to a learning block and a reluctance to take chances. From these activities we were able to progress from straightforward visual recognition tasks, to the sequencing and reading of very simple sentences using flash cards.

Towards the end of each half term, when I raised the subject of the next gap in our work, Tariq would become confused about the days and weeks and his difficulties with sequencing and time became apparent. Perhaps, too, he could not bring himself to think about breaks in our work. At the approach of one half-term ending, Tariq sadly asked me, 'But what about our partnership?' It seemed that, in his mind, we had formed an alliance and perhaps it had been in the service of fighting his monsters and therefore giving him some mental space for learning. To help with his confusion about timing we drew a calendar and discussed the weeks when we would meet and the ones when we would not. The periodic checking of this calendar became an important issue at the beginning and end of some sessions.

SUMMER: TERM 5 AND AN ENDING

During this term some sessions were missed because of school activities and visits and it felt a little like a return to the beginning of my work when session attendance was unreliable. However, my 'alliance' with Tariq seemed to be firm enough to withstand these unexpected losses of sessions and there were only brief returns to the use of the plastic dinosaurs and other animals to act out aggressive phantasies. There were glimpses, too, of Tariq making what appeared to be reparative overtures towards some of these much-abused animals. Sometimes he handled them tenderly and seemed to want to repair them by gently placing small blobs of glue on their 'skin'.

After half term, I was suddenly told that Tariq's family were leaving for Egypt again and that my last session would be the 4 July. I had only four weeks to prepare for an ending to the work. We used his calendar to talk about how many more times we would meet. He expressed sadness at the forthcoming ending with me when he slid down the wall and said, 'but I like you' and in response to an enquiry by me as to how he might be feeling about the end of the term he said 'more than sad'. During the final two sessions Tariq got in a tremendous muddle about how many weeks there were left. He made poo-coloured paint and covered a sheet of sugar paper, which was of a very similar colour to the paint mixture. The paint disappeared into the paper and I wondered if he felt he or I were disappearing like the paint. He then used this paint to cover balls of plasticine, which had been kept in a plastic pot, and showed them to me. I remarked that he was leaving me with his smelly pooey feelings. When he added PVA glue to them they became even smellier and he held them under my nose.

At the end of our penultimate session Tariq helped me put away everything. He stood on the chair and reached down to receive everything from me and placed it carefully in the cupboard. During our very last session Tariq asked for my help with repairing his robots (clay models he had made). It was a 'partnership' and he wanted my help. We talked about the notebook, postcards and pencils I had brought and the possibility of writing to me via the clinic and perhaps drawing some pictures while he was in Egypt. He was very interested, tender and thankful but he did not help me put anything away and left without a backward glance. It appeared that Tariq had managed the ending well. He had been able to express his sadness, his confusion and he showed concern for his broken clay models. It would have been beneficial for the work to continue and attempts are being made to arrange this.

COMMENTARY ON CASE STUDY OF TARIQ

The case study of Tariq clearly illustrates the anxiety that often surrounds a child's learning and behavioural difficulties. This child's behaviour causes his parents a great deal of anxiety. Anxiety is also evident in the response of professionals to concern about his apparent failure to learn appropriate classroom behaviour or to make academic progress. Several different attempts are made to understand the nature of his difficulties and it seems as though the educational psychotherapist is given the case, almost out of desperation. The child appears to be overwhelmed by his aggressive phantasies. It is the educational psychotherapist's task to be able to bear the way he communicates them and to help him to feel safe by the use of carefully structured boundaries.

This provides a setting in which thoughtfully chosen learning tasks can be introduced. Tariq can act out his feelings about sudden changes in arrangements and become more in touch with the reality of these feelings. The educational psychotherapist observes closely and develops an understanding of what it is about some of the educational tasks that makes them feel so threatening. This enables her to build up a relationship with Tariq that can withstand some of the external difficulties imposed by school and family on the continuity of the work.

When writing the case study, the educational psychotherapist selects the areas she wants to write about in detail. Here, she gives an account of her use of careful observation of Tariq to aid her understanding of his internal world. He uses drawings, play, bodily functions and interactive behaviour to reveal the conscious and unconscious thoughts that influence him. Some of the aggressive behaviours and the encopresis are very difficult for both parents and teachers to deal with, particularly as they are often regarded as personal attacks on the adult most involved with the child. The therapist also understands the personal nature of the attacking behaviour, but she is able to tolerate it because she recognizes the child's need to have his internal world understood and contained. This is a major part of the therapeutic work and is thus dealt with in some detail.

Another aspect of the child's external world that may have been very important is the fact that he is one of twins. He appears to be carrying many of the negative aspects of the children's role in the family. He may also have very complicated feelings about the other who shared the womb with him and who is therefore profoundly important to him while being a focus of rivalrous and confusing feelings. The drawing he produces in response to a squiggle, after the return to therapy from a long break includes a 'large, swirling maze with two small boys trapped in the middle and a monster breaking through the perimeter'. The reader may wonder if there are possible interpretations other than the one suggested by the therapist and consider in what ways Tariq's 'twinness' is important in the work or may have affected his learning and behaviour.

In class Tariq's behaviour is extremely testing and indeed we hear that he is at risk of exclusion. It seems likely that some of his emotional disturbance is connected to rivalry for his mother's love (coming 'first' and 'winning') and therefore having to compete with peers for a teacher's attention may feel overwhelming to him. Furthermore, managing educational tasks seems to have become connected in his mind with winning or losing and he therefore avoids activities associated with learning.

We see how Tariq projects unbearable feelings very powerfully into others in an effort to get rid of them but also perhaps because he feels his communications only get heard if they are very forceful. His efforts to gain the attention of and enliven a depressed mother seem to be re-enacted in the classroom with his teacher. Perhaps, too, his 'bizarre' and aggressive behaviour also serves to elicit a predictable response from the adult. This might be preferable to feeling powerless and unconnected and gives him some sense of control. It is notable that, in the psychotherapy, Tariq, who was 'chaotic' with little sense of time or sequence, responded positively to opportunities for order and may benefit from a highly structured school day.

7 Ongoing Assessment and Techniques used in Individual and Classroom Work

INTRODUCTION

We have seen how the educational psychotherapists represented in the studies have their own particular styles of working and, of course, each child has unique characteristics and learning needs. There is, however, a great deal of common ground in the accounts of the work. By now the reader will have gained some understanding, from the studies and from the chapter on assessment, of the ways in which educational psychotherapists conceptualize their work theoretically and of techniques and approaches they use. Here we hope to draw together the salient points of the approach and to consider how the underlying ideas may also be helpful to teachers working in educational settings.

Educational psychotherapy is based on the belief that bringing the unconscious impact of learning into children's conscious self-awareness can free them to learn. We saw how, for the children in the studies, aspects of learning, including relating to the teacher, had become imbued with special meaning relating to earlier experiences. The studies illustrated how working through the feelings aroused in the learning process is a major part of the intervention.

The therapist engages the child in an interaction in which symbolic communication between them takes place. Winnicott (1971a, 1971b) called this 'the potential space' and went on to say that real psychotherapy occurs in the overlap of a child's and an adult's play. The case studies vividly illustrate this process and show how the relationship with the adult is highly significant in the work. Tariq makes moving reference to the sense of an important alliance when told of a forthcoming break in the sessions. 'But what about our partnership?'

Fundamental to the work, is making sense of the ideas and feelings that are associated with the area of difficulty. Educational psychotherapists look for clues in children's expressive activities, responses to direct learning tasks and their attitudes towards them. As they gain understanding they find appropriate ways of conveying this to children, either through words or through choice of activity. Educational psychotherapists are also able to use their knowledge about children to adapt teaching methods in ways acceptable to them and to suit their particular needs.

The stories of the work with the children therefore represent a shared journey of exploration where children develop the capacity for reflecting on their own responses in the context of a learning situation. In a sense, the work comprises an ongoing assessment, so while the initial assessment process provides a formulation, the therapist remains flexible in thinking, taking the lead from the child, their evolving relationship and the unfolding process in the room.

In this chapter we will consider components of an educational psychotherapy approach including the following:

- using theoretical frameworks;
- establishing a secure learning base for the child;
- providing a different experience of learning within a relationship;
- noting defensive behaviour in the learning situation;
- presenting educational tasks and adapting teaching methods;
- fostering self-awareness;
- exploring feelings indirectly through metaphor and curriculum subjects;
- understanding the importance of play.

A DIFFERENT EXPERIENCE OF LEARNING WITHIN A RELATIONSHIP WITH A SIGNIFICANT ADULT

A 10 year old revealed her distrust of adults in a drawing of her therapist early in the work. She depicted her smiling benignly but with devil's horns. The children in the studies had a long history of educational failure and troubled relationships with adults. Both Kevin and Tariq were initially unwilling to engage with the therapist in activities in the therapy room. As educational psychotherapists work largely through learning tasks and shared activities, preliminary work was required to bring the children to a point where this was possible. Winnicott (1971a, 1971b) said 'where playing is not possible, then the work done by the psychotherapist is directed towards bringing the patient from a state of not being able to play into a state of being able to play.' This refers particularly to mutual play.

Maria and Osman appeared to engage with the therapist in tasks but covertly avoided real participation and were afraid to have their own ideas. They, too, required a lengthy intervention to effect change in their attitude towards the adults teaching them. Schools increasingly recognize that insecure children take time to form a relationship with their teachers and that they may benefit from a system where teachers stay with one class group for more than a year.

Children bring their 'internal working model' (Bowlby, 1969) of significant relationships into the therapy room and the classroom – expecting a response that echoes early experience with a carer. Osman, for example, had no expectations that his therapist might be someone who noticed his feelings, understood him or would find a way of communicating with him. Maria continued for a long time to expect her therapist to abandon or forget her. Both children needed an experience of being with an adult who consistently challenged these expectations by responding in a different way to the one expected. Resisting the pull to mimic his earlier experience is tricky for the therapist because the child powerfully projects feelings into her. Paying attention to these feelings, however, gives important information about his past experience. In order to be clear about what she may represent for the child and his habitual responses to an adult, the therapist keeps a low profile and avoids imparting personal information that might influence his views.

Although she does not always share her observations about the transference with the child, the educational psychotherapist uses them to avoid replicating unhelpful interactions. Osman's therapist, for example, had to resist doing all the thinking and choosing for him. Maria's therapist needed to notice and flag up small indicators of dissent and negative feelings in Maria who was so overtly compliant and idealizing of her. Kevin and Tariq both benefited from their omnipotence being challenged by an adult who created firm boundaries. Because the aim is always to give the children a new and different experience of learning to the one they had as infants, educational psychotherapy has sometimes been called 'second chance learning' (Barrett and Trevitt, 1991).

In school, too, teachers are on the receiving end of powerful projections from the children. Understanding that the interaction between herself and a pupil is affected by the transference makes it easier for the teacher to tolerate feelings such as rejection, hostility or lack of engagement and enables her to keep out of the conflict and reflect on the meaning of his behaviour. Furthermore, a teacher who sees how aspects of children's personalities in the class are allocated to individual pupils may be able to help children free themselves of these projections. For example, the class bully may need the teacher's help in being in touch with his vulnerability.

Teachers find that individual pupils elicit particular responses in them. They may feel highly protective towards one child, didactic and punitive towards another and so on. They also find that different children stir up particular feelings such as anxiety, irritation, fury and confusion. Attention to the countertransference can helpfully inform them about feelings with which the children may be struggling. It is helpful to remember that the way teachers respond to a child is also affected by their own personal history. One teacher felt so enraged by a 'contemptuous' boy that she found it hard to have him near her at all. When she was helped to link this with her feelings towards her father who had treated her with scorn and derision, she regained a capacity to reflect upon the reasons for her pupil's behaviour.

Winnicott considered that a teacher's more remote relationship with a pupil is an opportunity for working through important emotional issues and conflicts in relation to significant adults. Teachers can bear the expression of hostility and being disliked in a way that may be more difficult for a parent. In addition, the availability of curriculum subjects for expressing and exploring emotional issues is a powerful tool.

CREATING A SECURE BASE

Bowlby (1988) described 'a secure base' provided by a mother who is reliable and thoughtful. The securely attached child will be able to separate from his mother sufficiently to allow him to explore his environment. He trusts the adult to protect him from environmental impingements and to support him in managing powerful feelings so that he can turn his attention to toys and activities. In Chapter 3 we described how securely attached infants in the Strange Situation Test were able to be quickly reassured by a mother after an absence and to resume exploration of the room.

Educational psychotherapists hope to establish such a secure base for the child in their room – a place where the child feels safe enough to explore and take risks. The regularity of the sessions, the confidential setting and the therapist's predictable and consistent behaviour all help to foster the necessary trust and attachment. Boundaries around the session are strictly maintained so that the child has a sense of a safe place in which to experiment with new and different ways of learning and relating. The children in the studies demonstrated uncertainty and anxiety in their early educational psychotherapy sessions. They expressed this in different ways, such as hyperactive or withdrawn behaviour but common to all was a need to take control because it was too risky to trust the adult. Over time, as they increasingly experienced their therapist's reliability they were able, to an extent, to respond to her agenda. For some children this can take a long time.

The use of a box to store the child's work, symbolically emphasizes containment and continuity. He can be certain that his materials and creations will be looked after and protected in his absence. A child who is helped to distinguish between what is shared with other children who may use the room and the contents of the box for his unique use also gains a sense of a particular space for him in his therapist's mind. The contents of the box containing drawing, writing and modelling materials as well as books, games and completed tasks emphasize the juxtaposition of creative and educational activities. The box is offered to the child at the beginning of the educational psychotherapy and he is given the opportunity of making it his own through colouring it, putting his name on it or decorating it in some other way.

It is worth considering the importance for a child in school of having his own 'space' whether it is relatively symbolic such as a locker or a desk or room that they feel is their own. This can be particularly relevant for children making the transition to a secondary school where the move to different rooms throughout the day may leave them feeling rather lost. Many children who are competent learners are nevertheless drawn to small special-needs units within school where they feel safer and more contained.

In order to function well academically and socially, the child in the classroom must feel safe and secure. A major part of this, of course, will be children's feelings towards the teacher and whether they see them as capable of managing the group and responding to their needs. The uncertainties of school life can make it hard to maintain routines and boundaries but much can be done to foster a sense of safety. Examples of this would be awareness of the impact that changes and transitions may have on a child. Children may benefit from an acknowledgement that they dislike having a supply teacher or they may worry about whether their usual teacher is all right and will return. They may also need to be reminded about the order of the day and prepared well in advance for holiday breaks.

Unstructured time such as breaks and free time may need careful planning for children who need structure. Peer relationships need close monitoring too. It is important that teachers are entirely consistent and predictable in their own behaviour, remembering that some children are hypervigilant towards the teacher's state. They need to be aware of pupils who are hyperaroused or withdrawn and who may have difficulty regulating their own states. The child who fidgets when asked to sit on the carpet with other children may manage better if asked to sit near the teacher.

Sometimes, children need 'time in' when they are bought closer to the teacher rather than 'time out.' For insecure children the latter can echo previous experiences of abandonment.

CONTAINMENT

Bion (1962a, 1962b) said that the capacity to think arises out of an experience of being thought about. Through the mechanism of projective identification, infants let their mothers know about their feeling state. Mothers receive these communications, make sense of them and convey their understanding to the infants. For instance, they may soothe the children when they are frightened or feed them when they are hungry. When she can accurately reflect on his psychological experience in this way, her responses validate the child's perceptions and the children gain a sense of self, of agency and a belief in the capacity to anticipate events correctly.

We saw in the studies how educational psychotherapists need to be sensitively empathic to children and open to the full impact of their emotional states without being overwhelmed by this. At the same time they step back to observe closely and reflect upon the nature of the difficulty. It is important that children have a sense of someone who 'feels' their state and can bear it. Making sense of and naming the children's feelings helped the children in the studies to feel safe and form attachments. In a sense the therapist is using her knowledge of early emotional and cognitive development to recreate conditions essential for learning. Therapies that mimic developmental processes can be highly beneficial to children who have missed out on vital early experiences. For example, Osman's therapist recognized his need for a nurturing environment that would be appropriate to a younger child.

Teachers in school who can be curious about a child's behaviour and who think about its meaning provide containment. In particular children need to know that hostile and negative feelings are acceptable. It is clear that the worry about aggressive impulses often gets in the way of learning. Tariq's therapist tells us, for instance, how Tariq refused to read because he 'did not want to let the words out – as if they were in danger of becoming attacking objects.'

Melanie Klein (1931) emphasized the importance for children of feeling that both loving and hostile feelings are accepted and tolerated by the mother. She believed that in his phantasy the frustrated infant makes hostile attacks on the 'bad' mother. He needs repeated experiences of a mother who remains benign in order to reach the stage of ambivalence – that is, to cease splitting and to accept that the good and bad mother that he has previously kept separate in his mind, are one and the same person. This helps him to be more comfortable with his own hostile, aggressive feelings. We saw how Maria needed a great deal of help to integrate the 'witch' mother and the idealized mother. As stated earlier in the book, Klein suggested that the mother's body represented a treasure house of knowledge and that in order to take food for the mind from it, the infant needs to believe it is unharmed.

One child, highly anxious about his own aggressive impulses had a difficulty with breaking things up or taking things apart. This passivity impacted on his capacity to decode words or information. Underlying the difficulty was a belief that he had irrevocably destroyed his relationship with his mother through his aggressive feelings towards her. He was helped to overcome this inhibition by being enabled, in the safety of the therapy room, to dismantle and rebuild construction toys, jigsaws and eventually words which he cut up and stuck together again.

Teachers can help children to feel that their negative feelings can be borne and tolerated at the same time as indicating that there are appropriate and inappropriate ways of expressing them. Encouraging the use of books, writing, competitive games and other expressive materials that implicitly accept and recognize aggressive feelings is one strategy. Maria's therapist, for example, helped her to express negative feelings through the metaphor in identification with the wicked witch in her stories and also through 'beating' her therapist in board games.

Teaching reading and spelling through games such as 'hangman' is helpful to some children. The child hangs the adult by adding a part of the body each time he correctly reads a word. In doing so, he is able to express hostility towards the therapist symbolically at the same time as learning. Hangman can be useful in other ways. For instance using whole sentences in the hangman game can be a way of conveying an important message to a child. One child for instance refused to listen to her therapist when she attempted to tell her how many sessions were left before the end of term. She successfully guessed the sentence, which was 'We have four times together before the Xmas break.' Uncovering this piece of information herself gave her a sense of control and lessened the impact of having an unwelcome truth forced on her. Another means of conveying information in a tolerable way is through the use of puppets. One boy who always sang loudly to drown out his therapist's comments, showed great interest in a discussion about his angry feelings, orchestrated by his therapist, between two puppets. The case studies in the book illustrated how helpful it was for the children to express oppositional or negative feelings towards the therapist that she accepted and survived.

Recent research has emphasized that a crucial factor in the successful relationship between mother and infant is not so much that the mother is always attuned to her infant – but that when there are disruptions to the relationship these are quickly repaired. In school therefore, the speedy resolution of incidents or confrontations with teachers is important for pupils.

Being open to the impact of the distress underlying children's behaviour is very challenging in the school environment and only possible if the teacher is well supported within the institution. An ethos that builds in 'space' for the teachers to reflect upon and share with other staff their responses to children is vital. The authors of the studies were helped in managing their own feelings and providing 'containment' for the children through support received in supervision. Personal psychotherapy sessions also helped – particularly in separating their own responses from the children's.

THE EDUCATIONAL TASK

The use of structured imaginative activities and the learning task is one of the distinguishing features of educational psychotherapy. No conventional teaching programme is followed and tasks are chosen specifically for the child. This is very important because, as mentioned above, educational psychotherapists can ensure that the work they do is appropriate to children's emotional developmental age and to their very particular needs. The structured nature of a therapy that involves directed 'work' alongside free choice can be helpful to fragile children.

Activities that do not always appear to be 'educational' can be important learning tools. One educational psychotherapist, working with a child who was highly resistant to reading, was able to help him considerably through her use of jigsaw puzzles. He had revealed a difficulty in using the textual context as an aid in reading. The therapist noticed that when attempting to complete the jigsaw he again focused on individual pieces making no use of contextual information on other pieces or the completed picture on the lid of the box. When she suggested to him that he might look at the picture for help he said that that would be 'cheating'. The therapist realized that when reading the child believed that 'guessing' using clues such as initial letter sounds and context was somehow prohibited. She discussed this with him in terms of the puzzle and the concrete example enabled him to understand the link with his reading difficulty.

Interestingly, this same boy had been told that his aunt was his mother. Material in his sessions suggested that at some level he was aware of this secret and was quite afraid of looking at the 'whole picture' in relation to his family. As described in the assessment chapter, the question of what a particular aspect of learning means to the child is central to the work. This example illustrates the way in which the task, in common with creative activities and play, can be a vehicle for working through emotional conflict. Helen High (1985) points out that it can be particularly revealing to offer the child the opportunity to express his feelings at the moment when he is most anxious in the learning task in order to understand the underlying ideas.

The task can be very valuable in providing a mutual meeting ground and as a distance regulator for children who may feel threatened when alone with an adult and without a structure. Many children who would find child psychotherapy too threatening benefit from this. Adolescents often prefer a way of relating to an adult that decreases the intensity of direct communication. Avoidant children, too, respond particularly well to a therapy that includes a task acting as a 'buffer' that enables them to control the degree of intimacy with the therapist. Furthermore, avoidant children tend to respond positively to a task-centred approach because having had *predictably* rejecting mothers, they have greater faith in cognition and are therefore more likely to engage in a learning activity.

ADAPTING THE TASK

Teachers are well aware of the difficulty some children have in relation to persevering with a skill long enough to master it or to accept the inevitable gap between ignorance of facts and knowing them. They also see that some insecure children find it unbearable to wait for attention and help. These children may have experienced intolerable levels of frustration as infants and not had their needs met adequately. Winnicott (1971a, 1971b) described how the 'good enough' mother is closely attuned to her infant – sensitively protecting him from impingements from the environment until he has the maturity to manage the emotions aroused by an experience. By letting the world in little by little the infant learns to manage gaps in care and tolerate frustration. A child like this will later manage the frustrations inherent in learning. The educational psychotherapist who can accurately assess a child's emotional maturity and what he may or may not find bearable can plan her teaching accordingly. She gauges the degree of frustration that the child can manage at this point – so that learning is not experienced as intrusive or frightening – and uses this understanding to plan teaching, which is adapted in such a way as to ensure an experience of successful mastery of skills. Teachers in school have an extra challenge in that they must deliver the National Curriculum at the same time.

Caspari (1980) drew an analogy with the feeding situation where a mother provides food in a palatable way to the infant. She felt that introducing learning in ways that are 'digestible' to the nonlearning child is vital to the success of the intervention. She gave an example of this when she discussed a boy whose oppositional feelings interfered with learning. His therapist devised a game of 'opposites', wherein he could express his oppositional feelings while he learnt. Tariq's therapist found that he was more open to tasks and activities that gave him a sense of autonomy.

Rivalrous children sometimes respond well to two-way tasks that put the therapist on an equal footing. Educational psychotherapists find that the use of a die can be extremely important in this respect. Luck, rather than skill, is a leveller and the child does not have to face up to his inferiority in relation to the adult. Using two or more dice in board games and other activities can also be a helpful way of practising addition in the service of beating the adult.

Teaching through games can be particularly helpful with a child who is hostile or rivalrous because aggression can be expressed in a safe way within the rules of the game. Often games are structured in such a way that the child scores from the adult's mistakes. The child defeats the teacher by learning rather than not learning (Holditch, 1995). If the adult can demonstrate that aggressive feelings can be borne, a child will feel safer to be curious and exploratory and will attempt to make sense of the world.

Also a child can experience an adult as someone who can bear losing and does not become retaliatory.

Some children find it possible to communicate traumatic experiences and anger within the safety of a game. One child, for instance, used the questions in a board game to speak about her sexual abuse. She had been unable to discuss this subject outside the safety that the strict rules of the game offered. At one point, early in the work, Maria was too anxious to 'play' Hansel and Gretel but was able to do so within the safety of the board game that her therapist made.

Making learning tasks meaningful to a child is of fundamental importance. When teaching a child to read or spell, for instance, words that are significant to him should be the starting point. Children can help the therapist make cards or board games featuring words that they have chosen themselves. Pelmanism is an excellent game to play with a child who has good short-term memory and it can be adapted to any level of spelling/reading ability. Word bingo also has the advantage of putting the therapist and child on an equal footing. The child can use the words he chooses to learn to construct a crossword or a word search that the therapist must solve. In a similar way mathematics can be taught in a way that seems relevant to the child's world. Buying and selling in play, or games such as Monopoly, can be popular. Monopoly can be especially useful for a child who envies the therapist's 'treasure house of knowledge' because the child can accumulate valuable properties at her expense.

The use of a child's own work as his reading material can give him a sense of achievement. We find that children of all ages enjoy enacting scenes in the sand box, perhaps because of the tactile nature of the medium. This can give the therapist an opportunity to record the story he is enacting. Typing this up and presenting it to him in the next session in an attractive form conveys the value placed on it. This is particularly helpful for the child who is anxious about reading unknown texts.

In school, carefully selected educational activities can help children academically and emotionally at the same time. One teacher faced with a highly oppositional, low-achieving group of adolescents, chose to stage a play reading of an adapted version of *Billy Liar*. The play contained a great deal about conflict and ambivalent relationships between young people and their parents and much of the language in it was colourful and rude. The youngsters engaged enthusiastically with this and spontaneously made links with their own experiences. Some reluctant readers began to see written text more benignly.

The teacher was struck by the power of the curriculum to resonate with children's experiences in ways helpful to learning. The group was generally aggressive towards teachers but in this play-reading activity their hostility could be expressed through the content of the play in identification with rude Billy – and not towards her through misbehaviour and nonlearning. Of course the teacher needed to be aware that the task might just as easily work the other way and resonate unhelpfully with internal factors. Bettelheim gave an example of an adopted girl who became disruptive and distressed when the science lesson was about genetics. The teacher, not able to make sense of this, missed the opportunity to help her to think about the meaning of her response.

Teachers observe their pupils' responses in the classroom and can do a great deal to accommodate their needs and adapt their approaches even though the effect on the group always needs to be considered. Whole-class discussion of issues can be highly beneficial to children who have difficulty owning feelings but can recognize them in others. Individual needs can be addressed quite subtly. For instance, children who rely heavily on a sense of self-sufficiency should not be given a task for which they are not developmentally ready and some children who need to feel in control benefit from being given two choices within a task. A child who finds it hard to complete work may need to be offered open-ended ways of working.

Being part of a large group can be particularly difficult for some children. In order to have their needs met they must make a powerful bid for attention or otherwise fall in with the rest of the group. Kevin attempted to have his needs met through bad behaviour when he was in a mainstream classroom. Children who are very competitive with peers or cannot wait their turn need a great deal of support. Teachers can organize their teaching methods accordingly. For example overly competitive children may work better if they are not given the same project as the next child.

In planning their teaching approach teahers also need to consider the child's preferred style of relating to them – as described in the section 'Attachment Patterns' in Chapter 3. We saw there how 'avoidant' children may benefit from tasks that are presented in such a way that a child can find things out for himself and work independently of the teacher. A 'resistant' child on the other hand would need to know that a teacher was on hand and connected to him. Short tasks with built–in contact with the teacher might suit him best. 'Disorganized' children would benefit from a highly structured and predictable school environment.

DEFENCES GETTING IN THE WAY OF LEARNING

Teachers are aware that much of the behaviour observed in the classroom represents an attempt to manage painful feelings around learning and relating. In presenting an educational challenge the educational psychotherapist can observe defences a child uses in formal learning situations to cope with the anxiety aroused.

All four children in the case examples behaved defensively when faced with challenges in the classroom and clinic. Kevin, for instance, adopted an omnipotent stance, knowing everything already and being in control. Winnicott (1971a, 1971b) talked about an infant's need to experience a phantasy of omnipotence early on, through sensitive maternal attunement, before he is sensitively and gradually disillusioned. Kevin had lacked such an experience and had never learned that it was safe to rely on others. Tariq projected destructive feelings into his monsters and was then preoccupied and persecuted by their imagined retaliation. Osman shut out thinking through mindless repetition of activities. Maria denied aggressive feelings towards her therapist.

It is likely that all these children lacked an environment as infants where they felt contained and secure in their attachments. We heard how both Maria's and Tariq's mothers suffered postnatal depression, Kevin's mother was a drug addict and Osman was cared for by a succession of 'hopeless' minders. The infant who is not emotionally 'held' may experience a feeling of 'going to pieces' (Winnicott, 1990) or 'nameless dread' (Bion, 1962a, 1962b) and fear disintegration. He seeks to find ways to manage these unbearable feelings and defend against psychic pain. Psychological defences used may include splitting, projection, denial, omnipotence and regression. Anna Freud (1948) importantly extended and developed her father's work on defences and demonstrated how their excessive use militates against healthy emotional and cognitive development. These are explained more fully in the glossary.

One boy who had suffered chronic early trauma wrote a story that reflected his experience of premature exposure to a hostile environment. 'There was once a man who loved flowers. He went to smell one – and it bit his head off!' Not surprisingly his defence was a total lack of the capacity to be curious about the world.

Winnicott pointed out an additional danger concerning defences. When a parent sees a child, not as the child is, but as the parent expects the child to be this may be the basis of a great confusion for the child who may then develop a 'false self'. Osman's therapist was sensitively aware of this when she described the way in which he complied with her around activities she introduced early in the work. She said, 'He was going through the motions of playing but was too frightened to have his own ideas.'

METAPHOR, THE CURRICULUM AND EXPRESSION WORK

Caspari (1980) felt that curriculum subjects contribute to children's emotional stability and offer opportunities for the child to come to terms with problems such as aggression, violence, depression, sadness, jealousy and other emotions. History, for example, is about how the past impacts on the present. It deals with war and conflict and the struggle for possession and supremacy. Geography raises questions about race, culture and belonging and the way that the environment impacts on people's lives. It is also about distribution of resources. Science, too, is about who we are, our origins and about cause and effect. Mathematics, of course, is about relationships and about absolute certainty. It is also about loss and gain and sharing. Literature is possibly the most useful subject for exploring emotional issues.

As seen in the studies, educational psychotherapists choose to work mainly through the metaphor. These are sometimes spontaneously generated by the child and sometimes introduced by the therapist. The indirect exploration of issues can be particularly helpful to children who are emotionally fragile, distrustful or party to family secrets.

Maria, for instance, who was harbouring an inadmissible thought concerning angry feelings towards an absent mother, was able to explore these through stories. Interpreting through the metaphor, rather than directly, gives an opportunity for safe exploration of conflicts, dilemmas and ideas. The metaphor can also be a vehicle whereby the therapist conveys her understanding of the child's dilemma. For instance, she may choose a story or game specifically related to a child's preoccupations. Like the educational psychotherapist, the teacher can look closely at the content of a child's work or the way in which he approaches tasks for clues about his inner world.

USING BOOKS AND MAKING STORIES

The case studies indicate how large a part reading books and creating stories plays in the work – as was discussed earlier in the assessment chapter. Literature provides a wealth of opportunities for expressing and exploring ideas and relationships. Bettelheim (1976) has written about how fairy tales in particular offer the potential for exploration of deep-seated unconscious wishes and fears.

Exploring aspects of experience metaphorically can offer a new opportunity to examine alternatives and find solutions to problems. Identification with the characters in a story allows children to try out aspects of their personalities not normally accessible. Kevin who lacks control over events, enjoys identifying with powerful potent figures. As already stated, an essential component for the use of stories in the work is that it takes place in the context of a safe and containing relationship. Being read to by a trusted adult can feel highly nurturing to deprived children. Tariq, despite his hyperactive tendencies, 'falls into a reverie' when his therapist reads to him.

Children's fearful responses to particular stories can give useful information about ideas that they may not yet be able to manage. Sometimes rereading these in the presence of a reliable adult can help. Osman, for instance, found that the repetition of the wolf story enabled him to be less overwhelmed by his fears of being devoured. His psychotherapist reminds us that Bettelheim saw the wolf in the story as a projection of the child's badness: a child's wish to devour and the possible attack on himself. The rereading of stories with an emotionally significant theme not only helps him to experience hostile and negative feelings but also, as Caspari said, gives him a means to convey these to someone else.

The educational psychotherapist's choice of stories offers both a means of conveying her understanding of the child's issues and an indirect way of helping him tackle his demons. The story of *Hansel and Gretel* helped Maria to process some of her fears around kidnap and abandonment and allowed her to express hateful feelings towards the bad mother in the person of the witch. As stated in the assessment chapter children's own choice of books can be revealing.

Shared story writing, where the therapist and child write a few words or sentences each, can be useful in a number of ways. For slow writers it can maintain the momentum of the activity. It allows the therapist to introduce ideas into the story that may challenge a child to consider new ideas and options. The process of making a story with another person is valuable in that it builds a memory of an interactive creative experience. Some children have never had the experience of creating a collaborative view of the world with a significant adult. In the normal way of things this would be an infant's experience with his mother. Stern (1985) said that these new experiences of 'self with other' are the building blocks of internal working models. The changes in children's habitual stories during the course of the psychotherapy can provide a useful means of assessing emotional growth. For instance, characters may become more benign and there may be resolutions of conflicts. Story making has proved a very efficacious method in working with children in group educational psychotherapy (Morton, 2000).

PLAY, GAMES AND LEARNING

As we said in the assessment chapter, playfulness and play are an integral part of the closely attuned attachment relationship between mother and infant. If adverse early experience negatively impacts on children's capacity for play or playfulness, their learning may be compromised. The case studies are as much about play as they are about learning and demonstrate how the two go hand-in-hand with healthy emotional and cognitive development. Play increases self-awareness and helps children get in touch with their deepest feelings. It strengthens a child's sense of potency and mastery over the environment. Play is also a precursor to learning in the sense that one object stands for another in the same way as a word stands for an object and it invests external objects with meaning.

In his writings about the use of the baby's transitional object, Winnicott (1971a, 1971b) linked play with the attempt to separate from the mother and gain a sense of identity. He called the transitional object 'a symbol of the union of the mother and baby at the time they are becoming separate in the baby's mind.'

Winnicott proposed that a child needs to play alone in the presence of the mother if a stable true sense of self is to emerge. She must be sufficiently unobtrusive for the child to forget her and focus on self-exploration that lies at the root of solitary play. He said that there were three conditions for the evolution of symbolic functioning in the transitional space between infant and caregiver. They are:

- A sense of safety associated with experiencing the inner world.
- An opportunity for the infant deliberately to limit concern with external events.
- An opportunity to generate spontaneous creative gestures.

Winnicott says that a child is able to do this when he can rely on the adult being available when 'remembered after being forgotten.' This trust is clearly important in the educational psychotherapy room. Osman's therapist wrote about the beginnings of Osman's solitary play where he was able, for the first time, to become absorbed in it in the safety of her presence. Tariq's therapist describes Tariq's chaotic and frightening solitary play with monsters. 'He did not invite my participation in this play and it seemed that it was my function to watch, to take in and not to be overwhelmed by it and never retaliate.'

Winnicott reminds us of the different stages in children's play – from solitary play in the presence of an adult as described above – through to mutual play. Caspari linked these ideas to learning. She further divided mutual play into a stage where the adult fits in closely with the child's ideas and a stage where the child entirely accepts ideas from another person into his own imaginative world. The latter demands an acceptance of external reality, without which, Caspari points out, the acquisition of basic skills would not be possible. This has clear implications for the interaction between therapist and child. The former must assess a child's readiness to accept her contributions into his play. Caspari said that learning could be seen as a further stage of mutual play, but with far greater demand on the child to take external reality into account.

An example of the first stage of mutual play is a girl who initiated role-play with her educational psychotherapist. The girl was to be the baker and the psychotherapist her assistant. In her role of baker's assistant the therapist was entirely directed by the girl and was not allowed to influence the events played out in any way. Only later in the therapy, when she had gained trust was the girl able to move to the second stage of mutual play where she could allow her therapist to introduce some of her own ideas into the role play.

In her paper 'Play and Learning', Caspari (1980) says 'In educational therapy the use of play and games can be linked with the area of the child's emotional disturbance, which is another factor that diminishes his ability to deal with external reality.' We saw many examples of this in the studies. Tariq, for instance, was invited by his therapist to paint a section of the picture of a monster each time he read a word correctly. This harnessed his anxieties represented by monsters in the service of reading.

Making sense of the child's spontaneous play is an important part of the work. Tariq's play with the monsters that crashed, died and spun out of control in disastrous ways demonstrated the disturbed internal world that he could only manage by externalizing in this way. Osman, when making a plasticine pram, made a moving reference to his own experience when he commented that people don't talk to babies.

MATHEMATICS

Winnicott (1986) suggested that there were three groups of children who might be identified according to the way they learned mathematics. These were:

- those who could start with one and build up their knowledge from there;
- those for whom mathematics had no meaning because they had not yet reached unit status;
- those who are able to manipulate mathematical concepts to an advanced level but without any clear recognition of the stages they may have passed through to reach this point.

Among those who have studied the first of these groups is Piaget. By observation and experiment he found that children pass through three main stages of development. He considered that in the first two years of life, they pass through a sensory-motor stage followed by a period of concrete operations between the ages of 2 and 11 years. He called the years between 11 and 15 the period of formal operations because he recognized that during this stage the child becomes able to think in a detached way without the concrete situation to aid problem solving. It was recognized that innate ability and an enriching environment affected children's capacity to pass through these stages and the speed at which they might do so. There have been a number of attempts to refine Piaget's thinking and to develop a more precise understanding of the way in which children's mathematical understanding progresses. The assumption in this has always been that the child has an innate capacity to develop this understanding and we need to consider whether this is always the case.

The third group has often been the object of curiosity among the general public and the subject of the interest of psychoanalysts and neuroscientists among others. S. Blakeslee and V.S. Ramachandran (2005) mention several people who, while having very limited ability in general, have been able to develop amazing computational skills. One of the possible explanations for this is the idea that a particular area of the brain, known to be necessary for the development of mathematical skills and labelled the angular gyrus has for some reason become enlarged, facilitating an explosion of mathematical ability.

A different although not necessarily contradictory explanation has been developed to link mathematical genius with early experience. Plank and Plank (1954) studied the autobiographies of several eminent people and found consistent evidence of the traumatic severance from the mother at a fairly early age. They suggest that this, together with very aggressive feelings toward the father, can allow the apparent certainties of mathematics to develop as an absorbing area of interest that compensates to some extent for their lack of satisfying object relationships. It is a split-off intellectual process. This is linked with a process described by Joan Symington (1985) in which she relates how a baby who is feeling that the mother is unavailable to him and fearing to experience a state of unintegration, will hold himself together by focusing on some sensory stimulus. She gives the example of a four-week-old baby focusing on a light when the mother is temporarily distracted and gives other examples of the ways in which a baby may attempt to hold himself together. One of the ways in which a slightly older child may do this is by repetitive games that do not signal the joy of mastery over something difficult but indicate the child's need to reinforce the belief that he can exercise control. There is a time in the work with Osman where he 'enjoyed using the Unifix cubes, but his main interest centred on building up towers of numbers and making staircases of 1 to 10.'

His therapist recognizes the importance of this to him and sees it as a way in which he can begin to build up a sense of himself. After a few weeks she introduces groups of six cubes and attempts to help him to see that there are different ways of making that number. Finding it difficult, he clings to his defence of wanting to repeat the same pattern until gradually he is able to use her help. Later in the work he is able to move on to games involving number bonds to 20 and his therapist notes that although at times he coped well with the number bonds, at other times he needed to go back to basics, counting out numbers rather than counting on.

The reverse of the circumstances in which the infant feels the loss of the mother was also found to produce great difficulty in learning mathematics. A variety of instances are recorded where the child, usually a boy, for reasons of medical necessity or other circumstance has become so attached to the mother that separation from her causes intolerable distress. Winnicott (1986) maintains that 'arithmetic starts with the concept of one' and for this to happen, it is necessary for the child to make a developmental transition. Starting from a state in which it is difficult for the child to differentiate himself from the primary carer and where he unconsciously feels discomfited by the closeness of the parental relationship, he has to make the transition to a position where he can tolerate the relationship between two others and think of himself as a separate unit.

Of the four children whose cases are quoted in this book, it is Maria in whom we see the clearest connection between her emotional development and her difficulty with mathematics. Her educational psychotherapist notes the over-close relationship with her mother that is apparent in her clinging behaviour when they come to the clinic. She has suffered early rejection by her mother and has experienced her mother's period of postnatal depression. She could be described as having an anxious attachment. At the beginning of the therapy, she is not able to see herself as a separate person and is thus confused about what numbers represent. Her therapist also links this with the changing numbers of people in the family as they come and go without preparation or discussion. During the therapy, Maria experiences a close relationship but is able to learn that separation from the other can be tolerable. She learns that her educational psychotherapist can predict the coming separations and can assure Maria of her being there after the breaks. Maria is also able to express some healthy aggression toward her and this is another component of the capacity to engage with mathematics.

Tariq can only recognize groups of two or three – perhaps representative of him and his twin brother or him and his parents. Osman has had a very difficult early experience and has not developed the capacity to think symbolically. In an attempt at teaching him the concepts of 'more than' and 'less than', his therapist helps him to form two matching rows of counters so that he can see who has gained more in the preceding game. She says that he was able to see at a glance that he had more counters but that even with one-to-one correspondence he could not understand that he had four more. She reflects on the difficulty, for a child who had struggled to understand the concept of one or oneness, of understanding the concept of more.

How can these difficulties be addressed?

Winnicott (1986) has an answer to this question when he says, 'In such cases you leave arithmetic aside and try to provide the stable environment that may . . . enable some degree of personal integration to take place in the child who has such immaturity.' This is what the educational psychotherapists in the case studies have attempted to do and what the classroom teacher can set up with careful and structured classroom management.

He also suggests that it is important to take seriously a child's attempts at making sense of number. Those who find it easy are confident in their knowledge that it is either right or wrong. It can then be very frustrating to find that the child seems not to be able to experience number in the same way. The capacity of the teacher to tolerate the confusion the child communicates to her when he is unable to understand is a very important tool in developing a sense of confidence in the child. He can begin to see the teacher as dependable and not overwhelmed by his difficulties and can gradually internalize a feeling of greater competence and self worth. This process that teacher and pupil go through is similar to the developmental process experienced by a mother and young child.

Beaumont (1998) describes working with several children for whom mathematics is a particular problem and who all exhibited separation difficulties. She considers that, in addition to the practical steps that can be taken to make mathematics accessible to children who find it difficult, such as making it practical in terms of concrete examples and relating it to everyday life, the child's emotional needs should also be addressed. This includes paying careful attention to the process that the child goes through in order to reach an answer and being positive about and interested in the way the child has found to do this. Another important strategy is to understand how the child's difficulties relate to his psychopathology or background. A child who has suffered traumatic loss may find the operation of 'taking away' particularly difficult and a child for whom 'sharing' has been intolerable in some aspect of his life, may find that that mathematical operation reawakens the feelings experienced in life and makes it a process to be avoided. Some gentle linking and understanding of the possible connections can sometimes help the child to bring the unconscious resistance into his thinking.

BUILDING A SENSE OF SELF

Engaging the child in shared imaginative activity gives him the experience of a shared and validated view of the world that he may not have had before. Quite often the insecure child lacks a coherent account of his experience and a sense of himself in relation to others. This may be seen very vividly in the descriptions of Tariq, Kevin and Osman. An important part of the work is to help children to observe their own responses and to create a coherent narrative for them.

Naming feelings and thoughts and noticing aloud what children are communicating through their responses, increases self- awareness and enables children to make links between their behaviour and feelings. This strengthens their sense of self and they gain an experience of containment arising out of being thought about and understood. As time goes by they are increasingly able to make sense of their own learning behaviour and to find words to convey thoughts and feelings. In school, a teacher's choice of activity or materials in response to a feeling or preoccupation that the child is communicating can be a powerful comment-in-action. For instance, a child suffering from loss may benefit from the class reading a novel containing that theme. For older children we have found books by Michael Morpurgo, Jackie Wilson and Judie Blume useful in these circumstances. Many of the classics also deal with important emotional themes.

Activities such as making time lines of the child's life, family trees and other such concrete means of building a picture of a child's life can be useful. These methods need great sensitivity when used in a classroom setting where the teacher may know less about a child's home situation. One year 7 girl refused to return to school because her first project there was to write 'My Life Story.' Her life had been full of turmoil, disrupted relationships and abuse.

Most significant in building a coherent narrative for children is 'reflecting back' an accurate picture of them. The educational psychotherapist remembers Winnicott's words (1971a, 1971b) when he posed the question 'What does the baby see when he looks into his mother's eyes?' He suggests the child sees himself reflected there. The reader will remember a poignant response from Osman who looked into a real mirror and said he saw his father there. The therapist, in thinking aloud about what the child is doing or feeling, needs to hold in mind that if used to excess this technique may be experienced by the child as intrusive.

In this chapter we have attempted to summarize aspects of educational psychotherapy and therapeutic teaching. Caspari (1986) commented on the difficulty of conveying a real sense of a therapeutic intervention through describing techniques or theories. We hope, however, that the case studies, in conjunction with these descriptions, give the reader a clear picture of the work.

8 Case Study of Kevin, an Insecure Child Among Unpredictable Adults

This study, written by Claire Warner, clearly illustrates the impact of an unpredictable and traumatic home life on a child's capacity to learn. In particular Kevin, who might be considered 'resistant' in attachment terms, feels the need to remain highly vigilant to dangers in the outside world – including in the classroom – and cannot withdraw his attention in order to focus on learning. We see how his expectations of adults who cannot keep him safe are imported into the therapy room where the challenge for the therapist is to help him feel secure enough to relinquish control and to accept her teaching agenda. Engaging Kevin in mutual play is a necessary preliminary to formal teaching. The study also illustrates the power of the network around the child to help or to hinder the work. The trainee educational psychotherapist's own struggle to shift to a new way of working is vividly portrayed.

INTRODUCTION

This paper is about a boy called Kevin and the process of the educational psychotherapy that took place over two years. It is also in part a record of the process of training as experienced by the writer.

Kevin was seen at a CAHMS clinic that was part of a health centre housed on one of the most deprived estates in an already disadvantaged borough. The referral for Kevin had come through the Social Services and his school. There were concerns about the management of his behaviour both at home and school. He was also failing to make progress in his learning. When Kevin was referred for educational psychotherapy, a clinic worker was already seeing him with his grandmother. She was providing behaviour programmes for Kevin and individual support for his grandmother.

FAMILY BACKGROUND

The family background revealed a pattern of intergenerational abuse and poverty, necessitating substantial social services involvement. The family history included members of at least two generations being taken into the care of the local authority, special educational needs, violent crime, suicide and drug abuse. Kevin's mother became a registered heroin addict and he was born with withdrawal symptoms. His grandmother applied for 'control' and Kevin was made a Ward of Court. When the educational psychotherapy began, he was living with his grandmother and mother. His father was in prison but regularly absconding and Kevin had witnessed him 'shooting up' and violent fights between family members. Kevin's grandmother was in poor health and finding it very difficult to assert her authority with him. A source of support seemed to be her daughter and son-in-law for whom Kevin was considered to have respect.

At this time Kevin had recently transferred to the junior school from the infant school, where his grandmother had established a good relationship with the female Head. His new Head was a man with a 'no nonsense' approach and Mrs Jones (Kevin's grandmother) was unhappy about Kevin's progress. The school staff were also unhappy with Kevin and felt that he was unable to perform without the constant supervision of a primary helper. His behaviour at lunchtimes led to frequent exclusions.

Prior to meeting Kevin I observed him in his classroom and it was clear that he could not get engaged with his work; he fidgeted, fell off his chair, fiddled with pencils and moved around the room. He had more ways of balancing on a chair than I had seen at the circus. Yet his behaviour was really only disrupting himself. This changed when I saw him in the playground. He had no idea how to join a group and chased around barging into smaller children and picking fights. The school was hoping to begin a full assessment of his educational needs. The teachers considered him a non-reader although his grandmother felt he had learnt to read in the Infants but had now forgotten.

It was decided at the clinic that Kevin would see me for educational psychotherapy while his grandmother would continue to receive support from her social worker and the clinic nurse Caroline who was designated as my co-worker. Mrs Jones continued to see Caroline both at home and at the clinic, with and without Kevin. The social worker, Leroy, made home visits and took responsibility for ensuring Kevin's attendance for appointments at the clinic. I was to see Kevin in the room used by the specialist teacher at the clinic. This room was well equipped with books, sand, games and cupboards but had recently been redecorated with the addition of an enormous desk and executive swivel chair that took up much of the space. On the desk, were a computer and a printer.

TENTATIVE BEGINNINGS

TERM 1

Kevin was seven and a half when I first met him and tall for his age. He was a stocky boy but also chubby. He had light brown hair worn close cropped and an earring in one ear. His face had a flattened look to it and was invariably decorated with bruises and scratches. He alternated between a puzzled expression with his eyes screwed up or a sulky pouting look, which transformed him into a podgy toddler. He was always smartly dressed and usually heavily wrapped up in warm clothing with hat and gloves giving him the impression of being well defended.

Caroline, the co-worker, had met with Kevin and Mrs Jones to arrange the sessions and recommended that I begin with two assessment meetings. Due to difficulties in communication between the various people involved these two sessions happened over two months. As I sat waiting for Kevin before our first meeting I felt some excitement but overwhelmingly I felt nervous, feelings mirrored I imagine by Kevin in the waiting room. I was armed with my course notes on 'the first session' and full of plans to complete a full educational assessment. I never did find out Kevin's reading age. When Kevin entered the room he said, 'Is this your bedroom. I mean room?' Later I asked him why he thought he had come and he said quietly, 'to learn'. He was preoccupied with my appearance at his school and repeatedly said, 'I knew it was you.'

I played a letter game with him and he knew some letter names but no sounds. I was beginning to feel panic at my inability to complete any assessment as Kevin either covertly or directly refused to cooperate. Reflecting back on that first meeting, the themes of the two years that followed were already present. Kevin chewed gum constantly and towards the end, with reluctance, agreed to look at a book. He chose *The Very Hungry Caterpillar*, a very appropriate metaphor. He remained in some doubt about whether I could facilitate a metamorphosis and so did I. He asked if he could borrow the dominoes adding that Caroline, the co-worker, beat him at picture dominoes, thus revealing his confusion about our roles and his conflicting loyalties that remained throughout our work and mirrored his feelings about his mother and grandmother.

The second session contained the first expressive work Kevin did. Firmly wrapped up in his scarf and coat he ran through all the activities he might do, unable to settle for any. Whereas in the first meeting it felt as if he feared there would not be enough for him now he seemed to be in danger of being overwhelmed. He directed me to make a plate from the plasticine urging me to make it bigger and bigger. He was in charge of the food and created biscuits before moving onto the sand tray saying, 'I'm going to bury myself.' He buried his hand and then various animals under the sand, questioning me closely about 'other children's trays and special cupboards.'

As he was leaving he solemnly picked up the plasticine biscuits and pretended to eat them in turn saying, 'I have to take myself home – Gran's gone shopping'. Perhaps the look on my face prompted him to add, 'only joking' but to my dismay she was not in the waiting room and Kevin looked distressed. She arrived five minutes later, having been for a smoke but it was another portent of things to come.

TERM 2

Making use of supervision entailed a high degree of truthfulness, which seemed to evoke in me a flight to denial whenever possible but also offered the potential for empathy with the child. I didn't want to appear stupid or be a disappointment to my supervisor. I wanted to be an educational psychotherapist without learning how.

I felt deskilled and anxious, an impostor in this clinic full of people stuffed with psychological awareness and knowledge. I was caught up with my own anxiety and therefore unable always to see Kevin's. I had discussed in supervision the need to give the session some structure, as free choice seemed to provoke massive anxiety in Kevin. I decided on 'mine' and 'his' choosing times. I had in mind some educational projects I might initiate when we met again in January with the hope that we might make something together.

He arrived in good spirits but there soon began a period characterized by bargaining and boundary pushing. Could he take different items from his box home with him? He wheedled and cajoled, alternately pleading then hostile. I was seen as greedy to have all these good things in the room. I didn't need them all so why not give some to him, Kevin implied. Behind the behaviour there seemed to be fear and confusion. Was there anything of value for him here? I began to get used to reflecting back these communications and they diminished, always returning after a break. My attempts to introduce an educational task evoked great resistance and a blank, 'I can't do it.' These early sessions were marked by Kevin's need to feel in control in direct contrast to the rest of his life where he had no control. It meant, however, that he simply couldn't tolerate losing in games and after discussion in supervision, I tried to provide many opportunities for winning without colluding with him.

At this time the hardest thing for me as the trainee educational psychotherapist was to really receive Kevin's communication. I would get drawn into a conversational response or, faced with uncertainty, I would try to introduce an activity as in this extract:

> He brought the play dough to the sand and water, then put it in saying he wanted to see
> if it would melt. He dropped lumps of play dough into the bucket of water. Soon came
> the words. 'What can I do now?' I suggested I could read him a story but he replied very
> firmly, 'I don't like stories.' and then asked to go back to his Gran.

In the same session he had completed a story about a boy's three wishes. They were firstly to be good, secondly to have friends and thirdly to be nice to people. Kevin said he wanted to grow up because then he would be a man and he liked men. At first he said he had no early memory. I mentioned beginning school and he said, 'I was crying. It was new. I was frightened.' I made a connection between that memory and starting with me, and he nodded.

Kevin was still compulsively feeding himself with sweets during the sessions. Out would come a big bag of sweets followed by a smaller bag of gob stoppers useful for preventing talk. With his cheeks bulging he reminded me of a squirrel laying down his winter supplies. He still felt unsure about the nourishment available from me. Later on I tackled the issue of eating and the sweets remained in the waiting room. Just before the half term break Kevin began to make use of expressive work and many of the sessions were about messy play.

In March Kevin came into the room and expressed delight at the finger paints saying, 'Cor, yeah, what are they?' I explained that it was paint and you could use your hands and fingers to paint with. 'Oh yes, I know them', he said in a seen it, heard it, done it, tone ... Simultaneously, he was trying to remove the tops. He began by scooping very small amounts of paint into the tray, remarking that he liked how it felt. I suggested he might remove his coat and roll up his sleeves and he said, 'Yes, it's going to be messy,' with some glee. He copied me and rubbed some paint on his hands making handprints on the paper and progressed to mixing up the colours and making rainbow pictures. Soon there was more paint on his hands than in the pots. He was dripping with it and it was clear that he must use all the paint up. He experimented with scratching the surface and discovered streaks of colour underneath the thick purple. I remarked that he had found something beautiful underneath rather like finding the gold in the sand last week. He asked for some water and we moved to the sink and I filled it with water and fairy liquid. Kevin showed me how to blow bubbles and he became engrossed in water play continuing to make up rhymes with me and quietly saying, 'wishy washy.'

By the last session before the Easter break we both seemed to have relaxed. Kevin was beginning to trust me to be there for him and I was better able to recognize which feelings belonged to Kevin and which to me. The boundaries were clearer and I had met my initial aims.

TERM 3

There were two issues I needed to think about at the beginning of the summer term. Kevin and his Grandmother were supposed to be taking an extended holiday in America to visit Disneyland and relatives. Dates and duration were unknown and I was concerned that there might be a sudden break. From Kevin's return after the Easter break I was working towards this ending.

The structure that I had imposed in the session to give Kevin some security and boundaries now seemed to hinder the work. I wanted to be better able to respond to what he brought to the session because having preconceived tasks ready only served to restrict my creative response. The first two sessions were characterized by testing of boundaries and repetition of previous activities. Kevin read and reread *Where's Wally?* always trying to turn it into a competition that he must win. These sessions felt very uncomfortable and I was made aware of his anger over the break.

One day there was a great commotion from the room next door with much swearing and angry shouting. Kevin was transfixed by it but also became aware of the interconnecting door. I talked about how I felt about the noise and how he might feel but he was determined to find his way into the room. All my old inferiority anxieties about being an impostor in the clinic came flooding back, accompanied by the fear of losing control. To compound matters the door was opened from the other side and then closed. Kevin went over to the door and said he was going in. I said, 'No', but he went ahead and put his head round the door. Finding it, thankfully, now empty he was about to go further. I moved in front of him saying, 'No', again, closed the door and briefly explained why he couldn't go in. He immediately asked to return to the waiting room and ignored my reflections on his request. He seemed either unable to cope with being prevented from doing what he wanted, or fearful of retribution. His most frequent defence was through denial and omnipotence. He couldn't accept not knowing.

In one session Kevin had drawn a tree, a person and a house. The questions about the house had raised his anxieties about his real and imagined fears. His inner and external worlds were mirrored. In reality his home was not a safe place. He lived on a very rough estate and had been burgled several times. His natural father had broken into the house twice in the middle of the night and Kevin had witnessed drug taking and violent crime. Now he spoke of his night time fears, of being left alone and how his house needed more locks and bolts. He described the house in the picture as weak and if it could be said to represent the mother's body, then both his grandmother and mother were in poor physical and mental health.

Kevin had finally found an activity we could share without competition. I had brought to the session a pot of bubbles, which he used with great patience and concentration. We seemed to have arrived at the 'potential space' as described by Winnicott. Kevin had moved from playing alone in my presence to mutual play. He blew big pendulous bubbles that quivered and shimmered. He blew streams of little cascades and every so often he would blow the mega biggest balloon of all time. He made up names for them and carried on the rhyming game I had initiated the previous term.

Kevin always found the ending of sessions difficult and either tried to bring it to a premature close or tried to bargain for more time. During this term he found his own way of helping to manage the tension. He always chose to begin the session sitting in the massive swivel armchair. In one session I had reminded him that we had five minutes left and he had asked to stay for 10 minutes. I talked about how he might be feeling and Kevin said, 'I don't know what to do now.' Then he asked me to push him round in the chair. I did and he looked very relaxed and murmured baby talk to himself. I talked about him feeling giddy if I carried on pushing him in the same direction, linking it with when one can't think straight at school and you get in a muddle. (In between these sessions Kevin was regularly being excluded from school and it began to appear that the school would not fight to keep him.) He agreed and we changed direction. I felt as though I was rocking a rather large baby in a pram. Kevin lay back, gazing up at the ceiling with a soporific grin on his face. It was the first time I had seen his body and face lose its tightness. This regression became a pattern for sessions when Kevin felt reasonably centred but as the external pressures in his life increased over the next year he was unable to manage the endings at all.

We were now able to look at books together and Kevin would 'read' a book he knew and sometimes followed me in reading the text. He moved away from the tedious *Where's Wally?* and enjoyed the Willy books, in particular *Willy and Hugh* where Willy makes a friend and sees off the bullies. I was able to work, in the metaphor, at thinking about feelings and friendship. The other consistent activity was a game that had evolved from Pelmanism and Pan's game and in its present form involved a series of objects laid on the table. Kevin would hide an object and I would have to guess what it was and where it was hidden. Although we took it in turns, Kevin tolerated my go but enjoyed finding evermore complicated hiding places then assisting me with very obvious clues. On the one hand he wanted to win but he didn't want me to lose and he felt lonely being alone with the answer. The game was played with eyes closed but Kevin never managed not to peep.

Three sessions before the long break we were playing this game and I had my eyes shut when abruptly Kevin asked to go to the toilet. He went, but I had a sense that something was not right. The next week was the penultimate session, and the only thing Kevin wanted to do was repeat the game from the previous week. He began to wander around the room holding a monologue. I interrupted him sometimes to let him know I was still with him. He was talking in the third person – how he would be sad if I won and he had to make it very hard for me – how important it was for him to win. I connected this to the break and angry and sad feelings – 'yes, I am sad,' he replied. 'my ...' but didn't finish. Most of this time he was seated in front of a cupboard that contained stationery items and the door was obscuring him from my view.

Suddenly he asked to go to the toilet. On his return the game continued but now Kevin chose very quickly. Before he went to the toilet he had spent a quarter of an hour choosing. His shirt was slightly up and I could see two pens in his pocket taken from the cupboard. I suspect that this was also the reason for the toilet visit the previous week. Effectively, he wanted to stash his booty. I wasn't concerned with the moral issue but it did seem important not to let him go on his long break without exploring this issue. In a matter of fact voice when we were changing turns I said that the pens in his pocket needed to go back in the cupboard before he left. Kevin said he had got them from school and I showed interest but repeated that things in this room stayed here for him. I acknowledged how difficult it might be to leave the good things here behind and by taking something away it might feel like keeping a bit of the room but he could keep the good things he had done in his head during the holiday. He put the pens back and we talked about his mixed feelings; excitement about the trip but fear about the flight and sadness at leaving his Mum behind. The last session, before the break, was cancelled.

BEGINNINGS AND ENDINGS

YEAR 2

Kevin began the year faced with several unknowns. He had a new teacher and virtually a new beginning with me. However, the clinic was facing multiple losses with the redundancies of nine staff, over half the clinic and including the specialist teacher. At this same time my own job as a learning support teacher came under threat.

The full assessment of Kevin was proceeding and by midyear he was offered a place at a special day school for children with emotional and behavioural difficulties. His home circumstances changed significantly. His mother, Kerry, became pregnant and planned to move out and live with her boyfriend and her new baby. Mrs Jones's health continued to deteriorate.

Although I was now enjoying my work with Kevin and finding the experience of supervision immensely valuable I found the multi-disciplinary approach to this case frustrating and at times unhelpful. The arrangements for Leroy the social worker to bring Kevin frequently broke down without warning and communications between the co-worker and me were rushed. She continued to see Mrs Jones but also at one stage saw Kevin for 15 minutes, which he found confusing.

Kevin returned from the holiday physically bigger but felt like a much younger child and as with previous breaks I was made to feel his anger through his actions. I spent time linking up past and present sessions and Kevin began to make connections for himself. Taking the bubbles from his box he said, 'I've had these for a year.' He looked through his work, surprised that he had collected so much. Behind much of his behaviour lay the question, 'Have you missed me during this long break?' In retrospect, although not ideal, the long vacation did not seem as calamitous as I had previously feared. Kevin experienced that the clinic, the room and myself were all still there and unharmed.

The co-worker, Caroline, wanted to review the clinic's involvement. She was feeling less enthusiastic about her involvement with Mrs Jones who also seemed to have ambivalent feelings about the educational psychotherapy, which she communicated to Kevin. Caroline and Leroy held a review meeting, which I attended, towards the end. It was clear that Mrs Jones felt that Kevin was not making fast enough educational progress and was disillusioned with his school. By the end of the meeting she appeared to feel more positive about Kevin's sessions with me and agreed that it might be helpful for her to relinquish the direct responsibility to teach him to read. The education authority provided the school with a primary helper for Kevin every afternoon as an interim measure.

The Christmas term was marked by sickness. As the redundancies loomed nearer, sickness among the clinic staff multiplied. Kevin missed several appointments, when either Caroline, Leroy or grandmother were ill. He struggled to make sense of this in the sessions seeming forgetful and looking for explanations. He asked, 'Why didn't I come?' I reminded him that grandmother and Leroy had been ill. He asked if he could do some finger painting adding, 'How do you do it? I've forgotten.' He wanted to be reminded how many sessions we had been working together.

Kevin began to acknowledge that the room and things outside his box were shared with other children. This was linked to a new curiosity about letters and words in the room. In November, he asked what the name was on a child's tray: 'What does Danny begin with? That name begins with W. My name begins with K.' At the end of the session he noticed for the first time the sign on the door, which could be moved to read free/engaged. 'What does that say?' he asked. 'Engaged', I replied. 'What does that mean?' I explained. 'Leave it on engaged so people will think I'm still in there', he said. I explored in supervision how intrusive Kevin sometimes felt and how he might hope to really get 'inside' me. He could certainly get under my skin. In contrast to his usual act of bravado, the introduction of the puppet, Sweep, allowed Kevin access to his tender feelings as he cuddled it, sometimes communicating with me through the puppet.

It became increasingly arduous to maintain a 'secure base' for Kevin in the face of external events. His mother's pregnancy and impending departure from his home precipitated a reaching back to infancy for Kevin. On one occasion, he was preoccupied with finding a book he 'had read a long time ago'. It was about a cat who ate a lot and got bigger and bigger.

In the past Kevin had argued for more time but now he expressed a reluctance to attend and asked when he was finishing. On days when he shared part of his grandmother's session with Caroline before seeing me, he found it difficult to settle and was anxious about what was happening in his absence. He would 'forget' the name of whichever worker he wasn't with. As it grew closer to his ending at primary school he brought his mixed feelings into the session. He told me he hated the head teacher (the family felt he wanted to be rid of Kevin) and said that when people left they had to stand up in front of the class to say goodbye. He said he wouldn't do that – he would act like he was coming back and just say goodbye in the playground. He chose the story *Dogger*, about the loss and subsequent recovery of a favourite toy and sat curled up in the chair, his balaclava pulled over his face and a feeling of depression pervading the room. I reminded him that he would continue with me whilst at his new school but Kevin had not yet acquired the resilience and trust necessary to maintain hope. Yet the developments made during the first year remained. Kevin completed simple tasks of handwriting and making an alphabet book. He allowed me to read stories to him and was less controlling. He was even able to ask for help. He was beginning to show the ability to reflect on his feelings.

HANGING ON

When I caught up with Kevin after the Easter break he had begun to attend the day EBD school and his anticipatory anxiety of last term had been superficially masked by a veneer of 'hard man'. Kevin walked in with a newly acquired swagger and sneer, which prompted me to reflect that with so many tough things to deal with at the moment, perhaps it was hard not to be tough here. Later in the session Kevin and the swivel chair parted company causing him to fall to the floor. Immediately he laughed, and said 'That was funny.' I replied that I wouldn't think it funny if he was hurt. In this first session he went to the sand tray and talked about the skin that had formed on it since last term. I didn't comment but it seemed to me an apt description of Kevin's own present defence.

Much of the summer term was taken up with working towards the end and the sessions were full of challenging behaviour as Kevin did his best to finish with me before I could finish with him. He began to walk out of the room and on one occasion left the building. I recorded:

> Kevin took a long time returning from the toilet. I found Grandmother who said she thought he had returned to me. Kevin walked up the stairs carrying a bag of sweets that

he had just bought. I shepherded him back to the room where he grinned smugly at me. I said I thought he was trying to show me how unsettled he was feeling. He said he didn't have to stay and I said he might wonder if I wanted him to stay. I put a rug on the floor and sat down with a tray of Lego. Kevin remained high above in the swivel chair saying 'I'm not doing anything.' As I played with it, he joined me on the rug and asked me if I'd heard about this new bug, 'you get a sore throat, then you get scabs all over your face. It eats you up and then you're dead.' I said it sounded as if what he had heard had frightened him and he went on to relate car crashes he had seen and situations he was frightened of in his new school.

Kevin did manage to complete a papier mache model before we finished and in the final session he let me read *Amos and Boris* for the first time all the way through. We talked about how the animals felt about saying goodbye and how they would remember each other. He wanted to make a basket with a handle out of card and managed most of it for himself just asking me to reinforce the corners with sellotape. He took the basket away with him, an apt metaphor for the containment he needed to find.

SUMMARY

Towards the end of this case, Caroline, the co-worker, presented Kevin at a clinical review meeting. I was not informed in advance but nonetheless contributed an outline of my work with Kevin and my views on his future. It was decided that an urgent multi-agency planning meeting be held to discuss his future care as he was out of control at home and was at risk. Until his future was decided there would be no move to refer him for individual child psychotherapy.

I had found this a demanding and at times difficult training case. I was torn between writing up the work with Kevin or using my other case, a more straight-forward and superficially 'successful' case. But I learnt far more about myself, about the importance of boundaries and the complexity of working as an educational psychotherapist through my contact with Kevin. He, too, gained from the experience. Certainly he couldn't begin to learn whilst living with such massive uncertainties and the imminent loss of his mother from the home threatened his equilibrium. However within the small space we managed to create in the cluttered room, Kevin began to take what I had to offer. He experienced holding and containment over some time and rediscovered the capacity to play. He began to ask questions knowing that he would not be ridiculed or annihilated if something went wrong. He began to trust me.

I visited his EBD school in the final term and heard from his head teacher that he felt some optimism about Kevin. Although he saw him as a vulnerable child, wholly lacking in the social skills required to function within a group, he considered that with good planning and future psychotherapeutic intervention, Kevin would become engaged with his learning.

COMMENTARY ON CASE STUDY OF KEVIN

The account of the work with Kevin highlights the challenges of helping an insecure child to feel safe enough to learn.

Kevin's past experiences with significant adults are imported into the therapy room affecting his expectations of this new relationship. The family history suggests that his 'internal working model' might include interactions with unpredictable, unreliable and possibly frightening adults. The educational psychotherapist's awareness of this helps her to stay out of the conflict with him and remain reflective in the face of his rejecting, wary behaviour.

Knowing that Kevin has been faced with distressing events prematurely, she is careful to introduce new experiences at a pace and in a form that he can tolerate. She is sensitive to the way in which his need for vigilance and for staying connected to her, affects his capacity to focus on a task. She may also be aware of the neurological implications for a child who has been exposed to chronic trauma early in his development. Her appreciation of his level of emotional development enables her to be realistic about the aims of her work so that she holds on to hopefulness and optimism despite the limitations.

Current events in Kevin's life also impact on the therapy. The educational psychotherapist notes the way in which the lack of clear boundaries in the family is reflected in the network. She has contributed to this pattern by making an observation at the school. In the first session, Kevin confuses her role with that of the psychiatric nurse – just as he experiences confusion about his two 'mothers'.

The therapist is alert to the ways in which the desire to avoid painful feelings affect both her own and Kevin's behaviour. Both struggle with the difficulty of feeling unskilled. The therapist describes her flight into magical thinking in her desire to 'be an educational psychotherapist without learning how.' She arms herself with course notes in much the same way as Kevin 'arms' himself in his clothing and she resorts to flight into activity when faced with uncertainty or painful material. Kevin literally flees the room. Unlike her, however, he lacks the ego strengths to overcome these feelings without very considerable help.

Kevin adopts an omnipotent defence in the face of a world over which he has little control. Overwhelming feelings are projected into the therapist who is, for instance, to feel the shock of abandonment when Kevin says his grandmother is expecting him to go home alone. She is also the one who is to express greed – making larger and larger plasticene plates of food under Kevin's instructions.

As the therapy progresses and Kevin feels more contained he allows himself to be in touch with depressive feelings where he acknowledges loss and uncertainty. However with the deteriorating events in his outside world, when he is excluded from mainstream school and his mother becomes pregnant, he reverts to a 'hard man' demeanour. The therapist is sensitive to his need for this defence but gives a clear message that she can still be in touch with his vulnerability when she resists his invitation to find it funny when he falls off the chair.

In the counter transference the therapist experiences Kevin as keeping her out and rejecting her agenda or conversely, intruding into her and getting 'under her skin'. It is as if in Kevin's experience separating out comfortably from attachment figures has been very difficult. In his deprivation, he vacillates between viewing the therapist as someone with nothing to offer and someone bountiful who is greedy and withholding. His response is an attempt to be self-sufficient.

The need to defend against anxiety determines much of Kevin's behaviour when faced with learning activities. It is difficult for the therapist to assess his learning potential because he overtly and covertly avoids engagement with tasks. He resists moving on from familiar stories and attempts to divert the therapist from her agenda.

The therapist understands that Kevin needs to be helped towards engaging in shared play and that creating a 'potential space' in which she and Kevin can interact imaginatively, must precede formal learning. The messy paint play and bubble blowing seem an important step for Kevin. Not only is this mutual play but it also helps him to feel that messy, chaotic feelings are acceptable.

Kevin is a virtual nonstarter in literacy – although his grandmother has a sense of his having lost skills along with the loss of a significant infant teacher. It is in connection with Kevin's growing attachment to the therapist that he first shows an interest in letters and reading when he wonders about the initials of rival children coming to see her. As he becomes more trusting of her, Kevin is able to tolerate new stories and shows interest in texts that are personally meaningful. One of these, for instance, enables him to identify with a potent hero who 'sees off the bullies'.

By the third term into the work, the therapist is able to see that the structure (choosing time) that she had imposed on the work to reinforce boundaries, is now hindering her from creatively responding to Kevin's lead. This represents an important step in her learning where she relinquishes directive, 'teacherly' skills and adopts a more receptive, therapeutic approach. She is then aware of 'uncomfortable sessions' because Kevin has more opportunity to express his anger.

Whilst direct discussion of his experience seems hard for Kevin, he is able to convey a great deal metaphorically. Informed by her knowledge of his past experience and his current conflicts, the therapist provides him with opportunities for self-expression through a variety of creative activities. She is alert to the communications he makes. When Kevin draws a house/tree/person, his outside and inner worlds are mirrored, and he is able to express feelings about his unsafe environment as well as unconscious ideas relating to the state of attachment figures. Later in the work when he shares a catastrophic fear, describing the super bug that eats flesh, the therapist resists reassurance, taking up his scared feelings instead. The containment this offers enables him to talk directly about other worries concerning home and school.

Kevin finds endings and separations extremely difficult and deals with this by attempting to take control of them. In the sessions he bargains for more time or tries to end them prematurely. Eventually, in anticipation of a sudden ending at the clinic, he says he no longer wishes to come. When he tries to steal materials from the room, the psychotherapist understands that this relates to issues of loss, and handles the episode sensitively.

Kevin's experience of traumatic events impinging on his home life makes it likely that he will test boundaries at school to establish whether adults can keep him and the class safe. He would be highly vigilant to all that was happening around him with pupils and teachers and work may feel like an obstacle to this necessary activity. We saw in the sessions how when there was a disturbance in the next room Kevin's instinct for survival necessitated his investigating it despite his therapist's best efforts to reassure him. Furthermore the content of the curriculum might resonate with frightening undigested experiences. Because he lives in an unsafe environment over which he has little control Kevin clings to the belief that he is able to manage independently. It would therefore be important that tasks he is given are well within his ability until he gains confidence. Kevin would benefit from firm boundaries laid down by a consistent and reliable adult who establishes very clear rules and sanctions whilst acknowledging his need for defensive behaviours.

The educational psychotherapy with Kevin had to end while his external world was in a state of flux and uncertainty. Nonetheless his experience of the sessions had enabled him to make some progress. In his therapist's words: 'He experienced holding and containment over some time and rediscovered the capacity to play.'

9 Ways in which Endings and Beginnings Affect a Child's Capacity to Learn

Educational psychotherapists often refer to their anxiety about ending the work with the child. One said that she 'dreaded telling him about finishing. I imagined he would feel furious with me and refuse to come to the clinic.' In describing the last session with Osman, his therapist says 'I approached the final session with trepidation because I knew it would be difficult for both of us.' The difficulty experienced by her suggests that it may be even more difficult for the child.

It is interesting to consider what may be the basis of these feelings. Beginnings and endings are very much intertwined in their effect. Many of the feelings experienced by teacher/therapist and child are associated with their previous experience of starting something new and the feelings with which they were left when it ended. In the depth of the mind, there can be a powerful influence from very early experience. This can go back to birth and the extreme fear and helplessness created by the sudden need to take over the functions previously managed automatically in the womb and the dependence on others to play their part in this. The period of weaning can also be a time when a sense of loss and deprivation is pervasive because of the absence of a close physical relationship with the mother's breast.

Subsequent experiences that are well managed by the primary carer, such as trying a new food texture, being left with someone other than the usual carers, learning to put on your own clothes, can help the child to internalize a sense that difficulties can be negotiated and that adults will not leave you feeling humiliated but are there to support. Without this, we fear disintegration, and a loss of identity. With good internalized experiences, we are able to enjoy newness and to tolerate the sense of 'not knowing' that is a necessary part of being able to learn. Those who have not internalized good enough experiences may find new learning particularly difficult. Others, for whom this is a very unsettling time, include those who have had many changes of carer, who have had experience of traumatic separations or who have had recent experience of loss or separation.

The anxieties spoken of by the educational psychotherapists above may be partly an account of their own feelings but may also strongly reflect the way in which the child anticipates the beginning or the end of the work together. Approaching the end of the work suggests that progress has been made and that this achievement is a cause for celebration. This is very often the way in which endings are viewed within the school context. The urge to plan the curriculum as a series of targets, set and met, encourages the belief that this is the sole purpose of education. What can then be overlooked is the way in which relationships form an integral part of the work and the complexity of emotions that can underlie more overt behaviours.

TRANSITIONS IN SCHOOL

Planning for the period when year 11 pupils are taking their GCSE examinations and are then to leave school or go on to further studies in sixth form or at college has often exercised secondary teachers. They may feel that they have completed teaching the curriculum and that, without new teaching to interest them, pupils will become restless and unmanageable. Giving study leave to pupils who are beginning to seem more difficult to manage in school is often seen as a legitimate way of avoiding a potentially difficult situation. One of the difficulties for children is that they may be left feeling abandoned at a time when there is a particular need for structure and 'containment'. The familiar environment or 'secure base' of the school is suddenly withdrawn as a workspace. The study facilities and the teachers who have knowledge of both the pupils and the subjects they are studying are no longer available. Pupils may have little idea of how to 'revise' and may be left feeling that this is an impossible and lonely activity. If nothing is then put in place to offer a thoughtful and mature way of ending the year, the pupils are likely to deal with their distress and anger by some defence mechanism such as denying their sadness by wild hilarity and celebration or by projecting into symbols of authority their sense of being 'broken up' by literally mutilating their uniforms or school property.

Transitions also have a symbolic significance, combining recognition of both physical and emotional change, though, as with birthdays, the change is not always apparent on the identified day, but more often in retrospect. An earlier occasion when school children have to cope with an important transition is when they move from primary to secondary school. In areas where there are 'middle schools' the differences between schools are reduced but at whatever age there is a move from one school to another, the process can be difficult to negotiate. There have been numerous local research projects or initiatives that have aimed at easing these transitions but it remains the case that each child depends on their parents and the teachers in each school, as well as their own resources, to make it a manageable period of change.

It is also worth noting that individual transitions can be made more difficult if several coincide with each other. A five year old who is just entering the reception class at the local primary school, is moving house and is having to relinquish his position as an only child because of the advent of a baby sister may be, at least temporarily, overwhelmed by the collision of these events. It is also likely that his parents will be finding it difficult to give as much attention to his needs as they might otherwise wish to do.

The way in which the ending of one relationship is managed profoundly affects the individual's capacity to engage in further work. The experience of a manageable end to one piece of work can give confidence that it is possible to work through such an experience again and cope with the difficult feelings aroused. It also makes it more likely that the child can engage more fully in a new relationship because the destructive and painful feelings associated with the end to the previous one have been dealt with. Moving from one teacher to another at the end of a primary school year is also a time that needs to be carefully thought about and supported. There are also times when a number of people have been working together on a project and have formed a very close relationship associated with it. In school, this may be putting on a school play or concert, being part of a team taking part in a knockout competition or going away on a field studies trip. When the production is over, or the competition or trip is at an end, the participants can be left with a great sense of loss and real uncertainty about how to fill the gap. It is always important to acknowledge that there is sadness as well as excitement associated with the successful completion of the project.

EXPERIENCES RELATED TO ENDING IN EDUCATIONAL PSYCHOTHERAPY

Close relationships with parents, siblings, therapists or others, often give rise to very intense feelings. Most of the children whose case studies are quoted here, showed how those feelings were acted out in particular stages of the work and some of the ways in which the psychotherapists felt it necessary to deal with ending the work with each child.

It was important to make clear to each child that an ending was to take place. It could have been difficult for Osman's educational psychotherapist to separate Osman and his father when they were so closely identified with each other. Recognizing this, she takes an early opportunity to ask his father to wait in another room and thus indicates to Osman her confidence that he will be able to manage without him. Maria's therapist notes that the first break in their work came after only a few weeks. She says:

> It became clear, as we moved towards the first break, that Maria needed to know clearly why I would not be there, that I would be coming back and that I was not abandoning her . . . Maria had experienced loss and separation in her early life. I wondered if she would be able to trust me to 'be there' for her . . . Maria would ask, 'Where are you going? Are you coming back?' repeatedly. I found it hard to tolerate these painful feelings but it was not helpful to try to reassure her.

There is a mixture of anxiety and anger, which the children express when they realise that an ending is going to happen and they express it in a variety of ways. Maria shows her anger quite clearly when she says, 'You really want to get rid of me, don't you?' but her therapist is able to accept the comment. She acknowledges that it is hard to end and say goodbye and she adds:

maybe it felt as though I wanted to get rid of her, but that I would be there the following week. Later in the term I began preparing for the Christmas break. She immediately began splashing the yellow paint into the brown and then pretended to flick paint at me.

Kevin could not bear the tension associated with the approaching end of the session, so he either tried to bring sessions to a premature end or to negotiate an extension to the time. As the pressures on him outside of sessions became greater, he found it even more difficult to cope with endings. His therapist describes how he began to steal some of the resources from the session in a desperate attempt to hold on to the good experience he found there:

> The next week was the penultimate session, and the only thing Kevin wanted to do was repeat the game from the previous session He put the pens back and we talked about his mixed feelings; excitement about the trip but fear about the flight and sadness at leaving Mum behind. The last session, before the break, was cancelled.

Teachers in school often find that certain pupils regularly miss the beginnings and endings of term. Their parents appear to collude with their absences, by saying that 'they don't do much in the first/last week, anyway'. The long-term result of this seems to be that the child rarely becomes fully engaged with what is going on in the classroom. It is always helpful if their absence can be recognized and, if possible, they can be enabled to attend.

Tariq has a different way of dealing with his anger and the anxiety created by it. At the ends of the sessions he carefully controls the storage of the pictures he has created. He is very careful to impose order and cleanliness on the end of the session and his therapist remarks on the contrast this forms with his messy, uncontrollable soiling and stool hiding. In addition to this defensive procedure, Tariq projects into her some of the mess that he experiences as an internal feeling. He tells her that his cupboard is 'dirty' and, in a later session, when the ending is particularly sudden, suggests that she needs to wipe the walls, in a reference to old paint stains on them. The difficulty with 'projective identification' is that it creates a very worrying object and adds to the difficulty of returning for the next session. The therapist refers several times to the erratic nature of Tariq's attendance, but reflects that:

> while he appeared to hate being in the room with me he also needed to keep me un-contaminated and not participating – as if he had a story to tell and did not wish to be interrupted in the telling; to leave his horrors with me and to have me return unharmed the next week. I wonder now if his dislike and difficulty in returning each week was to do with fearing what damage he might have done to me and what retaliation awaited him.

WHAT HELPS?

A SAFE-ENOUGH LEARNING ENVIRONMENT

Educational psychotherapists acknowledge, throughout their work, that the relationship between therapist and child is a major feature of the potential for change in the child's functioning as a learner. They make clear, at the beginning of the work, that they will be available at regular times and in a particular place. They also make clear to the child that they will keep them both safe, in the sense that what happens in the sessions is confidential to them both and will only be divulged with permission or if she considers that the child has revealed that he or she is in danger. The therapist's regular presence and attention are predictable and dependable, although for some children it takes a long while for them to trust that this is so. One of the psychotherapeutic aims of the work is to create a sufficiently safe environment for the child to express negative as well as positive feelings.

The child in the classroom can also be greatly helped by the teacher's capacity to create a 'safe' learning environment. Well-ordered boundaries of time and space, together with a sense that the teacher knows what is appropriate for the child and can make a mental link with what has happened in previous sessions are powerful ways of being 'therapeutic' in the school setting. The adult's ability, in both the classroom and individual sessions, to tolerate being the subject of the child's phantasies and not to react unconsciously to the child's 'acting out' of inner feelings is also an important psychotherapeutic tool.

SYMBOLIC ACTIVITIES

If children can only cope with these feelings by acting them out defensively, they are in danger of being left with an unconscious fear that the feelings have destroyed the person against whom they were directed. If, however, the work with the child gives an opportunity to work through some of the more difficult feelings and to acknowledge the pain and distress associated with breaks and endings, there is a real chance of making progress. Osman's educational psychotherapist notes that he:

> became more able to tolerate separations . . . In the early stages he used the defences of shutting off and forgetting. When I talked about impending breaks he could not listen and when he resumed sessions he seemed to have forgotten everything that had happened previously . . . In the final session of the second term he spent a lot of time folding pieces of paper and stapling, gluing and sellotaping them together, as if symbolically enfolding both of us as a way of holding the memory of the session together.

Many of these kinds of activities can give a sense of reparation, both inside and outside the classroom. There is a section in the case study of Tariq, where the therapist describes the way in which, during the penultimate session, he carefully helped her to put away in the cupboard all the things he had made and used during their work together and was then able, the following week to leave her without apparent distress.

'Tidying up' is often regarded as a chore and adults – both parents and teachers – sometimes encourage children to see it as a punishment, and then collude with their wish to avoid it. It can, however, be a way of drawing together what has been done in a session or lesson. The act of putting away materials in a well-organized manner, conveys a sense that the activity is coming to a planned end and that there is an expectation that other work can be done on a future occasion. The most important aspect of this procedure is the care that is given to the written work, the models or the pictures that children have produced. Their work needs to have a place so that it can be preserved in the memory as something of value and can help to enhance not only their regard for the work they do, but also their sense of their personal value.

UNDERSTANDING FEELINGS 'IN THE METAPHOR'

Other elements of the curriculum can be very helpful in allowing children to consider distressing feelings 'at one remove' and therefore in a more manageable way. *Amos and Boris* by William Steig and, for older children, *Charlotte's Web* by E.B. White, are just two examples of stories that allow children to think about the experiences of sadness and loss without directly relating these feelings to themselves. Teachers are sometimes able to prompt sensitive discussions among pupils about the situations some historical characters have experienced. Other media, including films such as ET can provide the stimulus for a consideration of the sadness of parting.

WORKING TO A PREDICTED ENDING

The work of preparing for an ending requires a sustained period when the ending is anticipated but the difficult feelings associated with it can be contained within a safe physical and emotional environment. It is often the case that, in both clinical and educational settings, events can conspire to bring about a sudden end to the work with a child. Schools often arrange events at the end of term or offer the students the opportunityof working away from the school. Some children, or their parents, can suggest that 'nothing much happens at the end of term' and so can opt out of the last sessions. It is interesting to question why there is the urge to avoid these painful times but if the teacher or psychotherapist can acknowledge the importance of the ending, there is a better likelihood of negotiating these difficulties and insisting upon an appropriate end to the work with the child.

TEACHER MODELS 'HOLDING IN MIND'

The teacher or therapist has to be able to survive the anxiety which the child or group of children suffer as a result of the impending end. This experience puts them in touch with feelings of panic and chaos that they have earlier experienced when fearing abandonment by the adults in whose care they were. If the teacher or therapist can allow them to express their idealizing, denigratory, fearful or angry feelings and can allow them to recognize that they will miss the teacher/therapist, and if a record of work produced together, has been carefully preserved, this can form the basis of reviewing the shared experience. Thinking about what they have done together allows the children to feel 'held in mind' and gives them a sense that they can carry with them a memory of what they have experienced with this teacher or therapist.

TEACHERS' RECOGNITION OF CHILDREN'S DIFFICULT FEELINGS

If the teacher or therapist can acknowledge that perhaps the children are feeling anxious or angry and can attribute behaviours that exhibit this to the difficulties around ending, this also gives the child an experience of being thought about in a sensitive and calm way. The class teacher may no longer be teaching a class or may be moving to another school. The educational psychotherapist may not continue to work with an individual child. If these facts come as a great surprise to children they may feel that the teacher or therapist has been unable to bear their neediness and may experience the loss as a rejection. Thinking about some of the difficulties as well as the pleasures of moving on can remind the individual that painful experiences can be thought about. This then puts the child in a position where future relationships can be developed and the child can learn from them.

10 The Network – The Complex Task of Working with Parents and Professionals

There has been a growing recognition, over many years, that children's wellbeing and progress are promoted by good working relationships between the adults who have some responsibility for them. The ability of parents to consider the needs of their child and to work together in relative harmony is articulated by Brazelton (1992) as 'Babies don't need parents to agree. They learn very early to expect different things from each parent. What they do need is a sense of commitment from each parent and a lack of tension around them.'

This advice to parents might well be given to all workers with children but there also needs to be a recognition that it is often more difficult than expected. Language does not always offer the precise form of communication we would like it to and it often becomes clear that when responsibilities, thoughts and understanding about an individual child are shared among a number of adults, the resulting interaction can lose some of the dynamic quality of the child.

Educational psychotherapists working in CAMHS clinics and teachers and therapists working in schools have to find ways of working with parents, teachers and other professionals in the interests of the child. In this chapter we consider some of the issues that either promote or impede successful joint working.

ENGAGING THE PARENTS

Many parents find it very difficult to acknowledge that their child is having difficulties in school. They feel it is a criticism of their own role as parents and this can make them very defensive when teachers are trying to explore the child's problems. The teacher of the child described in the introduction, who is feeling overwhelmed by the child's behaviour and wants to tell the mother about it at the end of the day when she comes to collect him, may well seem a very overwhelming person herself. The parent feels put on the spot and expected to have an answer to the problem. Parents may also have found school a difficult place when they were children and find their resulting distress and anger reawakened when confronted with an apparently insoluble problem about their child.

If the teacher has been able to make some assessment of what it is that the child can manage and what it is that he finds most difficult about school and the expectations that are made of him, there will be much greater clarity about the concerns, for both the teacher and parents and also for other professionals who may become involved. Chapter 3 gives more information about this. Sometimes the anxiety aroused by a child leads parents or teachers to make referrals to a number of different agencies in the hope of finding an 'answer' to their concerns. One educational psychotherapist in training arrived at a CAMHS clinic to find two large files full of letters and assessments of the child with whom it was suggested that she might work. There had previously been an attempt to engage the family in ongoing work but this had failed. There continued to be attempts to make a firm diagnosis of the child's 'problem' by a variety of professionals but none seemed to give a clear picture of the child and what might be helpful to him.

Sometimes it becomes clear that the learning difficulty is serving a purpose in the family dynamic or that the parents have great difficulty in supporting their child's needs unless their own are in some way met. It is particularly in these cases that the school or clinic needs to work sensitively with the parents so that they are confident that the 'professionals' have something to offer their child but are also interested in them as people and not just as parents. Some parents who feel anxious about psychoanalytic approaches are more comfortable with a therapy for their child that has an educational focus. Thinking about their child's response to a task may be more manageable than thinking directly about the child's emotional needs. In this way the relationship between parents and other professionals can mirror the process of educational psychotherapy in that it deals with important emotional issues at one remove. At times, as in two of the cases quoted here, this can facilitate later child psychotherapy or other intervention.

We saw from the case studies how attempts to institute parent or family work alongside educational psychotherapy had varied success. If a child is being considered for educational psychotherapy in a CAMHS clinic there is already some recognition that the parents are hoping for assistance. The educational psychotherapist, therefore, will try to ensure that the child also receives dedicated sessions from another member of the team, so that the work with the child is well supported. All of the educational psychotherapists in training were able to have a family meeting and the support of at least one parent throughout the work. In the case of Maria, her therapist benefits from the previous involvement of the family with the clinic and her colleagues' insights into the family. She recognizes the anxious attachment between Maria and her mother but finds that the latter is committed to bringing Maria to sessions at the clinic. She is able to witness the growing independence of Maria and notes that her mother is ultimately able to express some annoyance at the continuing expectation that she will escort Maria to the clinic.

CONTACT WITH SCHOOL

Maria's psychotherapist made visits to the school both before the beginning of the work with her and then for visits each term. The purpose of the early visits to the school was to learn something of the teachers' experience of Maria within the school context.

There was then regular contact over the practical aspects of the work, so that the school was informed that it was ongoing and knew if there was any apparent breakdown in the work. The meetings each term were designed to discover any changes in Maria's functioning within the classroom and to give some feedback, not about the details of the therapeutic work but about the growing understanding that the therapist was gaining about Maria's needs and the ways in which she could be enabled to relate to others and to learn.

Kevin's educational psychotherapist, in addition to having discussions with the teacher, managed to observe him in class. This provided very useful information about the way in which he responded to a situation that, for him, provoked massive anxiety. However, a difficulty arose in her work with him because his hypervigilance in the classroom had made him aware of her and created further anxiety when he found that she was the person he would see in the clinic. In these circumstances it is important, not only to give a very brief explanation to the child but also to acknowledge that he may have been puzzled or be worried by the fact that the therapist seems to appear in two different places and to have different roles.

WORKING WITH OTHER PROFESSIONALS

Having a number of people working with a family can offer a very rich range of skills and the potential to increase the possibility of meeting a child's needs. Kevin's therapist finds, however, that at times there is confusion surrounding the roles of those working with the family and that, particularly when the workers are under additional pressure from the personnel changes in the clinic, some of the arrangements break down. In Kevin's case, the family had support from a social worker and the arrangements made at the clinic included the social worker's commitment to ensuring Kevin's attendance at educational psychotherapy sessions and the clinic nurse's designation as co-worker with Kevin's therapist. She was to work with Kevin's grandmother both at the family home and in the clinic. This highlights the importance of having a very clear structure for the work of a group of people who are all involved with one family. Both the family and the individual workers need to be clear about what can be expected of each one.

Winnicott (1965) gives some examples of the way in which professionals (he is speaking of doctors on this occasion) can be drawn into giving advice to parents about matters unrelated to physical disease. He points out that if professionals can hear about distress and other difficulties of family life, can contain them and allow a way forward to emerge from the airing of these problems they will have been more helpful than if they succumb to the urge to offer advice. He also notes that this will be more painful for the professional because it involves holding the problem without too quickly handing it back, repackaged, to the parents. There are particular areas on which each professional has specific expertise but blurring of the boundaries is likely to introduce confusion. Separating the place of contact, as well as the role, helps to define the work more clearly but it is also apparent from the work with Kevin that there needs to be time put aside for regular meetings of all those concerned. Kevin's co-workers have only 'rushed' meetings and, while this often seems all that is possible within the time constraints, it does not give appropriate value to the work each is doing.

The interface between professionals can create tensions that are not always articulated and, if not acknowledged by individuals, can have a destructive effect on the work. Stokes (1994) gives a concise account of the theory developed by W.R. Bion in relation to the functioning of groups. He reflects that, in a multidisciplinary team, it is important to recognize the interplay between the way in which the group approaches the 'primary task' (the task for which the group was brought together) and the way in which this is affected by the unconscious pressures often observed in the functioning of such a group. He notes that, 'when there is no clearly defined and agreed primary task, the tension between the professional identity and team-member identity of the individual is increased.'

He goes on to list some factors that he considers essential to the effective functioning of a team. These include a clearly defined primary task and a clear recognition that difficult or upsetting work is bound to cause anxiety. He refers to the role of management in supporting those who are involved in this type of work.

The complexity of the emotions that can be involved when a teacher is working with a child or a group of children needs to be recognized so that this can help the work rather than hindering it. Teachers have opportunities for discussing with their colleagues their work with children both formally and informally but this is not always found to be supportive. Any professional can feel exposed when thinking about an encounter that has been distressing. Gerda Hanko (2002) has been active in encouraging a joint problem-solving approach to developing ways in which teachers can think constructively about their work with particularly difficult children (and colleagues).

Tariq's educational psychotherapist seems to have had the experience of a group of professionals (some of whom are located in settings other than in the CAMHS clinic) but who are able to keep the child's needs in the forefront of their thinking and build up an understanding of his functioning. This enables them to develop appropriate provision for him and his family. His teachers have felt great concern at his behaviour in school and the fact that he seemed not to be learning. They involved the educational psychologist for the school who assessed his abilities and difficulties and developed some hypotheses about what might be the most important issues. Because there was a range of areas of difficulty including language delay and emotional and behavioural difficulties, a case conference was organized at school to consider which agencies might best meet the needs of the family. The task of the meeting was, therefore, clear, and a full assessment of Tariq's special educational needs was set in motion. Plans were also made for the family to have meetings with a family therapist to offer help with parenting skills.

Tariq is a child in whom is focused much of the anxiety of his parents and who inspires a number of different views in the minds of the professionals who become involved. Each sees him from the point of view of his or her own training and particular expertise. The school sees him as a child who is not learning and whose behaviour falls outside the normally accepted pattern. The educational psychologist is able to investigate specific aspects of the child's learning and to make links between his difficulties and some emotional factors. With further information about Tariq, a wider range of professionals is involved. The consultant child psychotherapist, from her experience of working with Tariq, suggests that more evidence is needed about possible neurological abnormalities that might be affecting his functioning. The consultant community paediatrician is able to give information about this aspect of Tariq and also to suggest that the history of his encopresis suggested an emotional and behavioural basis.

What is helpful here is that the school approaches Tariq's difficulties in a spirit of enquiry and has been able to use the help available in a way that is supportive to them and to Tariq and his family. When a child is so difficult to manage in school, it is very tempting to look around for anyone who will offer relief from the experience of being with him. Some agencies, then, find over a period of time that a child has been referred to a number of different services, as previously mentioned, and that the various professional opinions have not been coordinated into a coherent plan. The Common Assessment Framework is an attempt to create a structure that ensures that this situation will not arise. When referrals fail to produce the expected 'solution', it is often because the feelings of the professionals involved have been unconsciously affecting the work. These need to be recognized because even the most solid structure can be subverted by unconscious feelings.

DIFFERENCES OF VIEW

For parents bringing their child to school, there may be very mixed feelings. They may be delighted at the recognition that their child is ready to cope with school or anxious about the possibility that the child may have difficulties. They may also be sad that they will be missing out on some of the pleasure of seeing their child's new achievements at first hand or relieved that they will have more time free for their own interests. Teachers, too, have mixed feelings. The sense of rivalry between teacher and parent can be quite intense. Teachers may feel that they understand the child much better than the parents appear to do. They can also feel resentful that the parents have produced such a difficult child to teach.

When a referral to someone else for work with the child has been made, this can produce considerable envy on the part of a teacher. It sometimes feels as though this is an indication that the teacher's teaching skills seem to be in some way lacking and can imbue the other worker with very enviable qualities. By projecting their own sense of competence into the other worker, teachers can feel drained of it themselves. Then by a well-recognized process referred to as 'projective identification', they can wish to reject or disparage the quality of the other's competence and the insight that might otherwise be gained from it.

There is a suggestion in the work with Osman, that his therapist feels some disagreement with the child psychiatrist who 'did not wish Osman to attend family meetings'. She has obviously decided to go along with this decision but if the power to make decisions is vested too readily in one of the workers there can be destructive effects on the decision-making process. The differences need to be recognized and spoken about so that appropriate decisions are made with and for the child and family. The way in which the views of professionals are conveyed to parents is also a potential area of difficulty. To find their child labelled in a particular way can be very distressing for some parents.

Considerable sensitivity is needed in the debriefing following an assessment or when a particular professional's view of the child is communicated to parents, child or school. On the other hand, a diagnosis that is conveyed well to the parents can contain a person's anxieties in so far as it makes sense of the child's difficulties and behaviour. It may be unhelpful for children if, as they develop, the changes in their functioning fail to be observed and brought into a re-evaluation of their needs. It is part of the therapeutic process for children, if they are able to discuss with the teacher or therapist what they wish to convey to the adults in reviews, whether or not they are able to be present at the meeting.

It is clear that effective working within the network requires a great deal of hard work and thoughtfulness. The case studies illustrate both the helpful and unhelpful ways in which this can be managed.

11 Conclusion

In the last of the case studies, Kevin's educational psychotherapist gives some idea of the anxiety that can surround a professionally competent person who is trying to approach a task in an unfamiliar way. The experience of learning, at whatever stage of life, can be daunting and depends very much on the way in which previous learning situations have been negotiated. There are innumerable times when children in schools feel that they are not sure of how to do a task and that there is someone whose esteem they value but who may be disappointed at their efforts. Being able to articulate these feelings makes it possible to bring them into the learning process and gain a greater sense of agency. The children in the case studies are stuck at a very early stage of learning and so are unable to put into words the difficulties they encounter. They remain 'stuck' and unable to progress academically despite a considerable amount of special needs input within school. The case studies in this book and the supporting commentaries and chapters gave an account of a particular therapeutic approach that is increasingly being recognized as helpful.

The extent to which the intervention affected the children's learning positively depended partly on the nature and severity of their difficulties, the family and network around them and on the 'fit' between the child and educational psychotherapist. The work was challenging and, of course, not all the children were transformed by the process and residual difficulties remained. However it is true to say that the experience of educational psychotherapy left each of these children in a better position to make use of future teaching experiences and interventions. We hope that the reader was left with a sense of the important gains that all four children made in terms of self-esteem, the capacity to relate to the teacher and renewed hopefulness about achievement.

Teachers do not regard themselves as therapists but if they can find ways of helping a nonlearning child to learn they promote the child's mental health. When troubled children manage to master a new academic skill or to retain information that is seen as universally relevant, their view of themselves can alter radically. This is especially true of reading, which is so symbolic of entry into an adult world where individuals can access knowledge independently of others. Maths, too, is particularly important – and to some extent reliant on the ability to read.

As stated in the introduction, not all children can receive educational psychotherapy but they are all in a position to receive therapeutic education from their teachers in school. We hope that this too was illustrated in the book so that teachers may take away some of the theoretical ideas underpinning the approach and also some practical approaches that might enrich their work with vulnerable children.

For those teachers who would like to explore this way of thinking about children's learning difficulties and the way in which it relates to their emotional development, The Caspari Foundation (www.caspari.org.uk) offers a range of training courses including an MA in educational psychotherapy. Those who have studied this way of thinking, usually find that this unconsciously informs their approach to working with children in whatever educational setting. An educational psychotherapy approach does not preclude other educational interventions but can support them.

Glossary of Terms Used

Acting out   Expressing feelings, usually angry or anxious ones, through behaviour.

ADHD   A medical term relating to a cluster of symptoms including impulsivity, hyperactivity and poor capacity for paying attention. This is sometimes treated with medication. Can be difficult to distinguish from behaviours arising from traumatic past experiences.

Attachment   A relationship between two people that persists and is reciprocal. The attachment to caregivers in infancy is necessary to biological and psychological survival. Attachment is evidenced by proximity seeking and protest at separation.

Secure attachment arises out of healthy early interaction with reliable caregivers who can accurately reflect on the infant's psychological experience. It leads to a strong sense of self and confidence in the capacity to affect the environment. A securely attached individual will carry an expectation of others as benign and helpful.

In terms of child attachment classification originating from the Strange Situation Test, anxious attachment arising out of adverse early experiences with caregivers can be of three types: avoidant, resistant and disorganized.

Those who have had rejecting caregivers may be termed 'avoidant'. This child will attempt to be self-sufficient, be fearful of close contact and expect to be rebuffed by others. In school he may be reluctant to accept help from a teacher.

A child who has experienced an unpredictable caregiver may be called 'resistant' or 'ambivalent'. This infant will both cling and protest in an effort to maintain proximity. Later, in class, he is likely to be attention seeking but rejecting of the teacher in a directly hostile way.

A child who has experienced an adult who is frightened or frightening – such as those with mental health difficulties or who abuse substances, may be 'disorganized'. This child has not found a successful strategy to keep contact with his caregivers and may try a number of different ways to do this including bizarre or controlling behaviours. Such a child in class would be hard to manage because of his unpredictable and extreme behaviour.

Attunement   Being able to tune into another person's affective state using nonverbal communication.

Autism or autistic spectrum disorder   Characterised by poor capacity for understanding other people's thoughts and expectations. Such children tend to have difficulty in forming social relationships and may have weak psychological integration.

Coherent narrative   A clear story about one's own experience that makes sense and refers to real events and relationships and their emotional impact. This capacity to produce a coherent story about oneself is sometimes used as a measure of secure attachment.

Containment   Bion referred to the process whereby the caregiver holds or contains strong feelings expressed by the infant. This enables the infant to feel that these feelings can be tolerated and understood and are therefore not overwhelming.

Countertransference   This refers to the feelings evoked in an individual by other people. An example might be feeling a sense of gloom in the presence of a depressed person. The term can also be used to refer to feelings arising from one's own past experiences when interacting with another person.

Defences   The psychological attempt to protect the personality from attack or from overwhelming anxiety. A mechanism whereby painful feelings are kept out of conscious awareness. Anna Freud further developed her father's work on the way in which people use defences.

Denial   An attempt to block out unwanted knowledge and experiences from conscious awareness. A refusal to accept painful feelings.

Depressive position   Klein described this psychological state where a person can accept himself and others as whole people who have both loving and hating feelings. The individual who reaches this stage of emotional development shifts from preoccupation with self to concern for others. At times of stress people can vacillate between this state and a more primitive state.

Ego strength   This relates to the strength of the conscious part of the personality which mediates between instincts and outer reality.

Encopresis   Soiling that is not controlled and that occurs at an inappropriate age.

Enuresis   Urination that is not controlled. This can cause particular problems if it manifests itself through wetting the bed at night or in other social situations.

Epistomophilic instinct   This refers to the desire for knowledge. Melanie Klein wrote about this in relation to the child's feeling that the mother's body was a store of good things that could be given out or withheld. If a child believes that his hostile feelings have damaged the mother then he may be inhibited about taking what she offers. This feeling can subsequently be transferred to a learning situation.

Explicit memory   A memory that is available to consciousness and can be expressed in words. It includes autobiographical and narrative recall.

Fight, flight, freeze responses   These refer to the ways in which an individual may respond in event of perceived threat to survival. The three identified responses are to stay put and defend oneself, flee the danger or 'feign death' and remove oneself psychologically from the situation.

'Goodenough' parenting   A term used by Winnicott to describe a parent who can provide a facilitating environment for a child's healthy emotional development.

Identification   Freud described this in terms of the emotional tie between two people where one experienced an aspect of the other's personality as part of himself.

Implicit memory   This refers to a memory stored within the body but which is unavailable to verbal recall. The feelings associated with the unconscious memory of past events might resurface when individuals find themselves in a similar situation. For example a certain scent associated with an intense but repressed experience may reactivate feelings experienced at the time.

Individuation   A process by which a person begins to experience himself as distinct from others.

Indirect communication/metaphor   Exploring experiences through play, stories and the curriculum. This allows experiences to be thought about at one remove rather than through direct discussion.

Integration   Bringing together emotional states, experiences and behaviour to create a holistic sense of self.

Internalization   The process by which individuals take into their own psyche attributes or experiences of others.

Internal working model   Bowlby described the 'inner road maps' that children build about the world and themselves as a result of repeated experiences with significant others. These then form the basis of their expectations of relationships with others. These can be self-fulfilling prophecies because subsequent perceptions are selected to fit expectations.

Introjection   Freud described the process whereby an individual takes the attributes of another person inside himself. This can be used defensively when an image of another person is taken inside in an attempt to exercise control over the other. It can also be a helpful process when good objects are incorporated. For instance, introjecting a loving person leads to a sense of being lovable.

Mirroring   Responding to and reflecting back a child's feelings and thoughts to him through words or action. In early infancy a mother's capacity to reflect back feelings in this way is important to the child's development of a sense of self. Mirroring is a useful technique in helping a school child to feel validated and potent.

Omnipotence   An individual believes that being all-powerful is the only way of getting his needs met. Winnicott believed this to be a normal stage in an infant's development and it is associated with the paranoid – schizoid state. Omnipotence can become a problem if a child persistently uses this as a defence.

Phantasy   Unconscious ideas and thoughts often arising from early experiences of feeding and evacuation. These may later be unconsciously linked to learning experiences.

Potential space Winnicott's concept of the overlap between the world of fantasy and play and shared reality. This may occur when an adult and child are engaged in mutual creativity.

Projective identification A process by which aspects of self are expelled into another person or object. The person or object may then be seen in terms of the projected contents. For example if one has projected anger into another, that person may then be seen as aggressive.

Regression A defence whereby individuals revert to an earlier stage of development in an attempt to avoid difficult demands.

Repression The attempt to keep unwanted ideas and knowledge out of conscious self-awareness.

Splitting A concept developed by Klein whereby 'bad' feelings are split off. This results in aspects of feelings and experiences being kept separate and results in a lack of integration of the personality.

Sublimation A mechanism by which strong feelings may be expressed acceptably. For example rivalries may be played out in games.

Reparation Repairing the damage to others that an individual feels responsible for in the hope of preserving a good relationship. The fear of damaging another through hostile feelings can get in the way of learning when it results in the inhibited expression of feelings.

Transference The emotions related to early experiences with significant others are transferred to a person in the present – such as a teacher or psychotherapist.

Transitional objects Winnicott described this as the child's first 'not me' object which acts as a bridge between being merged with the caregiver and being separate from her but in a relationship with her. Children project onto the object (such as a toy, a blanket) the good relationship with the mother and this helps them to move to a state where they can hold the feelings associated with her in mind while moving to a greater independence.

Trauma An experience that has been overwhelming and cannot be integrated into a normal state of mind. The earlier the trauma the greater its lasting impact.

References

Ainsworth, M. (1985) Patterns of infant-mother attachments: antecedents and effects on development. *Bulletin of the New York Academy of Medicine*, **61**(9), 771–791.

Ainsworth, M.D.S. and Wittig, B.A. (1969) Attachment and exploratory behaviour of one-year-olds in a strange situation, in Foss, B.M. (Ed) *Determinants of Infant Behaviour*, Vol. 4, Methuen, London.

Balbernie, R. (2001) Circuits and circumstance: the neurological consequences of early relationships and how they shape later behaviour. *Journal of Child Psychotherapy*, **27**(3), 237–255.

Barrett, M. and Trevitt, J. (1991) *Attachment Behaviour and the Schoolchild*, Tavistock/Routledge, London.

Beaumont, M. (1998) One add one makes one: Some reflections on the emotional and social factors that affect learning in mathematics, in Davou, B. and Xenakis, F. (Eds) *Feeling, Communicating and Thinking*, Papazissis, Athens.

Bellack, L. (1949) *Children's Apperception Test (CAT)*, CPS, Gracie Station, NY.

Bettelheim, B. (1976) *The Uses of Enchantment: The Meaning and Importance of Fairy Tales*, Thames & Hudson, London.

Bick, E. (1968) The experience of the skin in early object relations. *International Journal of Psychoanalysis*, **49**, 484–486.

Bion, W.R. (1962a) A theory of thinking. *International Journal of Psychoanalysis*, **43**, 306–310.

Bion, W.R. (1962b) *Learning from Experience*, Heinemann Medical, London.

Blakeslee, S. and Ramachandran, V.S. (2005) *Phantoms in the Brain*, Harper Perennial, London.

Blanchard, P. (1946) Psychoanalytic contributions to the problem of reading disabilities. *The Psychoanalytic Study of the Child*, **2**, 163–187.

Bowlby, J. (1969) *Attachment and Loss*, Vol. 1, Attachment, Penguin, London.

Bowlby, J. (1988) *A Secure Base: Clinical Applications of Attachment Theory*, Routledge, London.

Brazelton, T.B. (1992) *Touchpoints*, Viking, London.

Buck, J. (1996) *The House-Tree-Person Technique: Revised Manual*, Weston Psychological Services, Los Angeles.

Caspari, I. (1980) *Learning and Teaching: The Collected Papers of Irene Caspari*, FAETT, London.

Davidson, D. (1988) Playing and the growth of imagination, in Sidoli, M. and Davis, M. (Eds) *Jungian Child Psychotherapy*, Karnac, London.

Freud, A. (1948) *The Ego and Mechanisms of Defence*, Hogarth Press, London.

Geddes, H. (2006) *Attachment in the Classroom*, Worth Publishing, London.

Hanko, G. (2002) Therapeutic joint problem-solving. *Educational Therapy and Therapeutic Teaching*, **11**, 57–67.

Harris, D.B. (1963) *Children's Drawings as Measures of Intellectual Maturity*, Harcourt, Brace & World, Inc., New York.

High, H. (1985) The use of indirect communication in educational therapy. *Journal of Educational Therapy*, **1**(1), 3–18.

Hodges, J., Hillman, S. and Steele, M. (2004) *Story Stem Assessment Profile (SSAP)*, Anna Freud Centre/GOS/Coram Family, London.

Holditch, L. (1995) Learning only a game? *Educational Therapy and Therapeutic Teaching: Issue 4*, 34–43.

Ironside, L. (1995) Beyond the boundaries: a patient, a therapist and an allegation of sexual abuse. *Journal of Child Psychotherapy*, **21**(2), 183–205.

Klein, M. (1931) A contribution to the theory of intellectual inhibition. *International Journal of Psychoanalysis*, **12**, 206–218.

Klein, M. (1975) *Love, Guilt and Reparation*, Hogarth, London.

Koppitz, E. (1968) *Psychological Evaluation of Children's Human Figure Drawings*. The Psychological Corporation, USA.

Main, M. and Solomon, J. (1982) Discovery of an insecure – disorganised/disoriented attachment pattern, in Parkes, C.M. and Stevenson-Hinde, J. (Eds) *The Place of Attachment in Human Behaviour*, Tavistock Publications, London.

Malchiodi, C.A. (1998) *Understanding Children's Drawings*, Jessica Kingsley, London.

Moore, M.S. (1990) Understanding children's drawings: developmental and emotional indicators in children's figure drawings. *Journal of Educational Therapy*, **3**(2), 35–47.

Moore, M.S. (1995) Reflections of self: the use of drawings in evaluating and treating physically ill children, in Erskine, A. and Judd, D. (Eds) *The Imaginative Body*, Whurr Publishers, London.

Morton, G. (2000) Working with stories in groups, in Barwick, N. (Ed) *Clinical Counselling in Schools*, Routledge, London.

Murray, L., Kempton, C., Woolgar, M. and Hooper, R. (1993) Depressed mothers' speech to their infants and its relation to infant gender and cognitive development. *Journal of Child Psychology and Psychiatry*, **34**(7), 1083–1101.

Perry, B. (1999) The memories of states. How the brain stores and retrieves traumatic experience, in Goodwin, J. and Attias, R. (Eds) *Splintered Reflections, Images of the Body in Trauma*, Basic Books, New York.

Plank, E.N. and Plank, R. (1954) Emotional components in arithmetical learning as seen through autobiographies. *The Psychoanalytic Study of the Child*, **9**, 274–293.

Rosenzweig, S. (1948) *P-F Study (Form for Children)*, NFER Publishing Company, Slough.

Schore, A. (1994) *Affect Regulation and the Origin of Self*, Lawrence Erlbaum Associates, Hillsdale, NJ.

Schore, A. (1998) *Affect Regulation: A Fundamental Process of Psychobiological Development, Brain Organisation and Psychotherapy*, Tavistock 'Baby Brains' Conference, London.

Sletten Duve, A.-M. (1988) The Norwegian educational assessment method. *Journal of Educational Therapy*, **2**(1), 1–11.

Stern, D. (1985) *The Interpersonal World of the Infant*, Basic Books, New York.

Stokes, J. (1994) Problems in multidisciplinary teams: the unconscious at work. *Journal of Social Work Practice*, **8**(2), 161–167.

Symington J. (1985) The survival function of primitive omnipotence. *International Journal of Psychoanalysis*, **66**, 481–487.

Thomas, M. (1937) Methode des histoire a completer pour le depistage des complex et des conflits affectif enfantins. *Archives of Psychology*, Geneve, **26**, 209–284.

Weininger, O. (1989) *Children's Phantasies: The Shaping of Relationships*, Karnac, London.

Winnicott, D.W. (1965) *The Family and Individual Development.* Tavistock, London.

Winnicott, D.W. (1971a) *Therapeutic Consultations in Child Psychiatry*, Hogarth Press, London.

Winnicott, D.W. (1971b) *Playing and Reality*, Penguin, London.

Winnicott, D.W. (1986) *Home is Where We Start From: Essays by a Psychoanalyst*, Penguin, London.

Winnicott (1990) *The Maturational Process and the Facilitating Environment*, Hogarth, London.

Index